Home Office Research Study 263

Alcohol, crime and disorder: a study of young adults

Anna Richardson and Tracey Budd

The views expressed in this report are those of the authors, not necessarily those of the Home Office (nor do they reflect Government policy).

Home Office Research, Development and Statistics Directorate
February 2003

Home Office Research Studies

The Home Office Research Studies are reports on research undertaken by or on behalf of the Home Office. They cover the range of subjects for which the Home Secretary has responsibility. Other publications produced by the Research, Development and Statistics Directorate include Findings, Statistical Bulletins and Statistical Papers.

The Research, Development and Statistics Directorate

RDS is part of the Home Office. The Home Office's purpose is to build a safe, just and tolerant society in which the rights and responsibilities of individuals, families and communities are properly balanced and the protection and security of the public are maintained.

RDS is also part of National Statistics (NS). One of the aims of NS is to inform Parliament and the citizen about the state of the nation and provide a window on the work and performance of government, allowing the impact of government policies and actions to be assessed.

Therefore –

Research Development and Statistics Directorate exists to improve policy making, decision taking and practice in support of the Home Office purpose and aims, to provide the public and Parliament with information necessary for informed debate and to publish information for future use.

First published 2003
Application for reproduction should be made to the Communication Development Unit, Room 201, Home Office, 50 Queen Anne's Gate, London SW1H 9AT.
© Crown copyright 2003   ISBN 1 84082 961 3
                          ISSN 0072 6435

Foreword

This study reports on some new analysis of the data from the 1998/99 Youth Lifestyles Survey (YLS), which has been undertaken to explore the relationship between alcohol use and offending. The YLS offers a unique opportunity to examine binge drinking and criminal and disorderly behaviour alongside other related lifestyle factors thus providing a more complete picture of alcohol-related behaviour.

In conjunction with the statistical analysis, data from in-depth interview with binge drinkers aged between 18 and 24 years of age are presented. These provide a more detailed examination of the experiences of young people who drink in busy entertainment districts. In addition, the young people were asked for their views on how to improve the drinking environment and ultimately reduce the prevalence of alcohol-related incidents.

The evidence produced by the YLS, together with the views of the young adults interviewed, indicate that alcohol-related crime and disorder, especially violent crime, is an issue that deserves widespread attention. Findings from this report should be of particular importance in informing policy development.

TOM BUCKE
Drugs and Alcohol Research Programme
Research, Development and Statistics Directorate

Acknowledgements

The authors would like to thank Professor David Farrington (University of Cambridge) and Professor Martin Plant (University of the West of England) for acting as independent assessors for this report.

Thanks are also due to colleagues from the Research, Development and Statistics Directorate and the Violent and Youth Crime Reduction Unit of the Home Office for their help and advice throughout this project.

In addition, we would like to thank Tiggey May and Alex Harocopos (Southbank University) and Andrea Finney (RDS) who undertook some of the fieldwork for the study. Thanks too are due to all those who gave up their time to take part in the research.

Anna Richardson
Tracey Budd

Contents

Summary

This report presents the findings of research into young adults, drinking and crime. In recent years there has been rising concern about the prevalence of drunken behaviour, especially among young adults, and associated crime and disorder. In response the Home Office has produced an Action Plan *Tackling alcohol-related crime, disorder and nuisance*. The plan identifies objectives and priorities for taking forward a programme of work to address the problem of alcohol-related crime and disorder. The research findings presented in this report provide an evidence base to inform policies relating to the reduction of alcohol-related crime and disorder.

Previous research indicates that the young adult age group is most likely to binge drink and most likely to be involved in crime and disorder. Taking this as a starting point this report describes the extent and nature of binge drinking and criminal and disorderly behaviour within the 18- to 24-year-old age group and examines the relationship between binge drinking and criminal and disorderly behaviour, including illicit drug use.

The findings from the nationally representative 1998/99 Youth Lifestyles Survey provide the statistical basis, while additional information collected from 27 in-depth interviews conducted in 2001/2002 with young adult binge drinkers provides contextual information about the perceived links between alcohol and offending and potential policy responses. The key findings are presented below under the relevant chapter headings.

General Drinking Behaviour (Chapter 2)

- Overall 97 per cent of 18- to 24-year-olds had drunk alcohol at some time in their lives, with 95 per cent drinking alcohol in the twelve months prior to interview.
- One-tenth of those who had drunk in the preceding twelve months drank every day or nearly every day of the week. A further two-thirds drank at least once a week. Around one-tenth drank once or twice a month and the remainder less frequently.
- The most popular type of drink for this age group was beer or lager, followed by spirits and wine. Alcopops were far more popular with women (29%) than men (12%). The majority of drinkers had consumed more than one type of beverage in the week prior to interview.

- A substantial minority of young people drank excessively. Twenty-eight per cent of 18- to 24-year-old men and nineteen per cent of women had drunk more than the weekly recommended amount. Among 18- to 24-year-olds who had drunk in the past twelve months, twelve per cent said they had felt 'very drunk' at least once a week.

- Drinking alcohol for this age group is a very social experience. Around eight in ten said they had been to a pub in the last month and three-quarters had been to a party, dance, night club or disco. The majority drank with friends (87%). Unsurprisingly, then, most young people reported that young people their age drank to be sociable with their friends (91%) and because they liked going to pubs and clubs (92%). Seventy-five per cent said young people drank to get drunk, 63 per cent to relax, 58 per cent to feel confident and 30 per cent because of boredom.

Extent of Binge Drinking (Chapter 3)

- Thirty-nine per cent of 18- to 24-year-olds were classified as binge drinkers (those who got very drunk at least once a month); 42 per cent were 'other regular drinkers' and 18 per cent had occasionally or never drunk alcohol. Males were more likely to binge drink (48%) than females (31%).

- Almost a fifth of binge drinkers reported drinking on nearly every day of the week. They were more likely to drink several types of alcohol and more likely to drink beer and spirits than other drinkers.

- A similar proportion of binge drinkers and other regular drinkers said young people drank for social reasons. However, binge drinkers were far more likely to report that young people drank in order to get drunk (86% compared with 68% of regular drinkers).

- Binge drinkers and other regular drinkers were as likely as each other to go to a pub. However, binge drinkers were a lot more likely to go to a nightclub, dance or party than other regular drinkers (91% compared with 77%).

- Data from the qualitative interviews broadly reflect the findings of the YLS. However, alcopops and spirits were found to be the most popular drink and drinking several types of drinks in the course of one evening was common.

Drug taking, crime and disorder (Chapter 4)

- Frequency of drunkenness is strongly associated with illicit drug use. Fifty-nine per cent of 18- to 24-year-old binge drinkers admitted taking illegal drugs compared with 33 per cent of those who drank regularly but did not binge.
- For all drug types, apart from LSD and heroin, 18- to 24-year-old binge drinkers were significantly more likely to admit use than other regular drinkers.
- Frequency of drunkenness remained a significant predictor of drug use even when other factors were taken into account. An individual had three and a half times the odds of taking an illegal drug if they got drunk at least once a week, compared with those who got drunk less than once a month. The relationship was particularly strong for cocaine and amphetamine use.
- Data from the qualitative interviews also indicated that those who drink alcohol quite often take illegal drugs, sometimes in combination. Most of the interviewees felt alcohol was more responsible for crime and disorder in the night-time economy than any drug, with the possible exception of cocaine.

Binge Drinking, Crime and Disorder (Chapter 5)

- Two measures of offending and disorderly behaviour were asked about in the Youth Lifestyles Survey. Firstly, respondents were asked about various offences committed during the last twelve months. Secondly, respondents who had drunk in the last twelve months were asked if they had been involved in specified disorderly or criminal activities during or after drinking alcohol.
- Frequency of drunkenness is more strongly associated with general offending behaviour than frequency of drinking. Eighteen to 24-year-old binge drinkers were almost three times more likely to have committed an offence than 18- to 24-year-olds who often drank but were infrequently drunk. This difference was particularly marked for fights: young binge drinkers were five times more likely to admit involvement in a fight.
- Multivariate analysis confirmed that even when other factors were taken into account frequency of drunkenness was still an important indicator of offending and disorderly behaviour. This was particularly apparent for violent crime. Eighteen to 24-year-olds who got very drunk at least once a week had five and a half times the odds of admitting to a violence offence than those who got drunk less than once a month.

- Frequency of drunkenness was also strongly associated with offending or disorderly behaviour during or after drinking. Binge drinkers were twice as likely to have participated in arguments during or after drinking, four times as likely to admit taking part in a fight, five times as likely to admit to criminal damage and eight times as likely to admit to a theft than other regular drinkers.
- Offending and disorderly behaviour during or after drinking remained strongly associated with frequency of drunkenness when other factors were taken into account. An individual had over four times the odds of committing a disorderly act during or after drinking if they got very drunk at least once a week.
- All of those who took part in the qualitative interviews had experienced or witnessed assaults or fighting while out drinking. The consensus was that alcohol was, at the very least, a factor in the majority of the incidents.

Reducing alcohol-related crime and disorder (Chapter 6)

- The young adults interviewed came up with various ideas to encourage more moderate drinking and to reduce crime and disorder linked with excessive drinking.
- Suggestions for encouraging moderate drinking included licensed premises offering soft drinks at cheap prices, bar staff refusing service to intoxicated customers, well thought out 'safer drinking' campaigns and the provision of alcohol education in schools from an early age.
- In terms of reducing crime and disorder the interviewees advocated targeted policing of busy entertainment areas, harsher penalties for those arrested for alcohol-related crimes, improved vetting procedures and intensive training for door staff, longer opening hours, plastic bottles and glasses and improved transport links out of town and city centres.

1.   Introduction

Alcohol use is rooted in many cultures and the vast majority of adults in England and Wales regularly consume alcohol. Drinking alcohol is for many people part of normal social interaction, results in no or few problems, and, consumed in small quantities, can even have health benefits for certain groups. However, when alcohol is misused it can result in difficulties for the individual and wider society. Harmful patterns of drinking are associated with physical and mental health problems, accidents and crime and disorder.

The government is therefore committed to developing a comprehensive National Alcohol Strategy by 2004.[1] A consultation exercise is currently being undertaken by the Cabinet Office's Strategy Unit with the aim of producing a final report by summer 2003, which will form the basis of the strategy. In advance of the launch of the new strategy, the Home Office has produced an Action Plan 'Tackling alcohol-related crime, disorder and nuisance'. The plan identifies objectives and priorities for taking forward the programme of work to address the problem of alcohol-related crime and disorder. The three key objectives are:

- to reduce the problems arising from under-age drinking;
- to reduce public drunkenness, and associated criminal and disorderly behaviour; and
- to prevent alcohol-related violence.

The plan sets out the key actions that are being taken to address these objectives.[2]

In addition, there is a joint, cross-departmental target to reduce the level of alcohol-related crime such that the level in 2005/06 is lower than in 2001/02.[3]

The research findings presented in this report provide an evidence base to help inform the development of policies to address the problems of crime and disorder arising from binge drinking. The research, based on new secondary analysis of the 1998/1999 Youth Lifestyles Survey (YLS) and in-depth interviews with 27 young people, focuses on young people aged 18 to 24 years. It explores their drinking behaviour and to what extent this is

---

1. As stated in the 1998 Green Paper and 1999 White Paper *Our Healthier Nation*.
2. A full copy of the Action Plan can be downloaded from the Home Office website: www.homeoffice.gov.uk.
3. Two targets have been set (i) to reduce the incident rate of alcohol-related violent crime and ii) to reduce the percentage of the population who perceived drunken and rowdy behaviour to be a problem in their locality. These will be measured by the British Crime Survey

associated with criminal and disorderly behaviour. More specifically, the research addresses the following objectives:

- to identify the extent of 'binge' drinking among young people, which groups of young people are more likely to engage in this pattern of consumption, and why young people 'binge' drink;
- to identify the extent to which young people become involved in criminal and disorderly behaviour during or after drinking alcohol;
- to examine whether 'binge' drinking is associated with offending behaviour; and
- to examine the links between 'binge' drinking and illicit drug use.

The findings from this report are complemented by further qualitative research, based on focus groups, designed to examine in depth the nature of young adults' drinking patterns and the social consequences, particularly criminal and disorderly behaviour. The findings from the qualitative study are published in, *Drunk and Disorderly: A qualitative study of binge drinking among 18- to 24- year- olds* (Engineer *et al.*, 2003).

Underage drinking is not explored in either report. For a discussion of underage drinking see Harrington, 2000 and Honess, 2000.

Structure of the report

The remainder of this chapter provides some further information about the study and places it in the context of the existing research evidence. Following from this:

- *Chapter 2* briefly examines the patterns of drinking behaviour among 18- to 24-year-olds, including frequency of consumption, amount consumed and the social context of drinking
- *Chapter 3* examines the extent of binge drinking among this age group and identifies those most likely to binge. It also explores motivations for binge drinking
- *Chapter 4* examines the association between binge drinking and illicit drug use
- *Chapter 5* explores the links between binge drinking and various forms of offending behaviour
- *Chapter 6* explores young adults' views on ways of minimising the harm associated with binge drinking
- *Chapter 7* provides an overview of the key research findings and the policy implications

Links between alcohol, crime and disorder

The relationship between alcohol, crime and disorder is complex. The evidence of an association is well documented in the research literature. Collins (1982) explored the relationship between alcohol consumption and criminal behaviour. He concluded that there is sufficient evidence to justify the inference that alcohol is sometimes causally implicated in the occurrence of serious crime. However, he stressed the need for continued empirical support for this assumption and advocated that all research should be based on sound explanatory understanding and be methodologically rigorous. Since then there has been continued debate about the nature and extent of the alcohol-crime nexus.

The British Crime Survey indicates that a third of violent incidents between strangers and a fifth of violent incidents between acquaintances take place in or around a pub or club. In half of all stranger incidents and a third of acquaintance incidents the victim considered the offender to be 'under the influence' of alcohol (Mattinson, 2001). Canadian-based research by Pernanen (1991) found that in violence occurring in bars and taverns drinking by both victim and offender was more likely than in violence occurring in other contexts. The BCS also indicates that a substantial minority (17%) of those who had been insulted, pestered or intimidated felt that this had happened because the perpetrator was drunk (Budd and Sims, 2001).

It is not possible to conclude from such evidence, that certain incidents of crime and disorder are directly attributable to the consumption of alcohol. However, it is clear that criminal and disorderly behaviour is a problem in the night-time economy[4] and that incidents are concentrated in and around pubs and clubs on weekend nights, particularly during the period immediately following the closure of licensed premises. For a summary of key themes relating to violence in the night-time economy see Finney (forthcoming). Moreover, much of the research evidence suggests that the 'binge' drinking culture, mainly associated with young adults, is particularly linked with crime and disorder. The following section discusses the phenomenon of binge drinking and its association with crime and disorder in more detail.

---

4. In this context the night-time economy refers to 'the commercial sector of an economy providing entertainment venues, particularly those serving alcohol and which are often clustered within town centre commercial districts' Finney, forthcoming.

Binge drinking

The term 'binge' drinking has gained currency in the alcohol field in recent years. Bingeing is broadly regarded as a consumption pattern that involves high levels of consumption over a short period of time.[5]

Evidence has suggested that intermittent, high consumption drinking patterns are more strongly associated with health hazards than regular, low-level consumption patterns. This is reflected in the 1995 Department of Health report, *Sensible Drinking*, which recommended daily rather than weekly guidelines for sensible drinking.[6] There has also been a shift, both from a research and policy point of view, to the acceptance that the amount of alcohol drunk in one session is a better predictor of alcohol-related crime and violence than overall consumption (Cherpitel, 1993; Shepherd, 1996; Deehan *et al.*, 1999).

Extent of binge drinking

An inherent problem in researching alcohol and, in particular, binge drinking, relates to definitional and measurement issues. There is no consistent, agreed definition of what constitutes binge drinking and how this can most accurately be measured (Murgraff *et al.*, 1999).

Several large-scale, nationally representative, government funded surveys regularly include modules on alcohol consumption, including the General Household Survey, The Health Survey for England and the ONS Omnibus Survey. While these surveys are not specifically designed to measure binge drinking, they do include questions which allow the estimation of the percentage of the population who could be considered as binge drinkers based on their pattern of alcohol consumption in the previous week.[7] Each of these surveys defines binge drinking as follows: *men/women consuming more than eight/six units of alcohol on any one day in the previous week* (see Appendix B). This equates to drinking more than double the recommended daily allowance. These sources suggest that around a fifth of men and just under a tenth of women could be classified as binge drinkers based on this definition.

---

5. Clinically, binge drinking is defined as continuous, dependent drinking over a day or more until the drinker is unconscious (Newburn and Shiner, 2001). In research terms it is more generally used to describe drinking to excess on one occasion. Alternative terms used in the literature include risky single occasion drinking and heavy sessional drinking.
6. Sensible Drinking: The Report of an Inter-Departmental Working Group, Department of Health, December 1995.
7. Each survey asks respondents on how many days in the week prior to interview they drank alcohol and how many drinks of various types they consumed on the last/heaviest drinking day in the previous week. Based on assumptions about the units of alcohol contained within standard drinks, the number of units consumed on the last/heaviest drinking day can be calculated.

Other unit-based definitions have also been utilised in the UK research literature, including half the recommended weekly intake (eleven or more units for men; seven or more for women). The Royal College of Physicians adopted ten units or more and seven units or more in their influential 2001 report 'Alcohol – can the NHS afford it?'.

Unit-based definitions have been criticised by some commentators because they take no account of important individual factors, such as weight, alcohol tolerance and, sometimes, even gender, which may affect the influence that alcohol has upon an individual. Similarly the effect of the social context in which alcohol is consumed, such as location, atmosphere, and presence of other drinkers, is not catered for in these measures (Midanik, 1999; Murgraff, 1999; Raistrick et al., 1999). Midanik (1999) suggests an alternative approach would be a more subjective measure of frequency of drunkenness.

The variety of definitions of binge drinking used in research makes comparisons of studies difficult. However, Appendix B summarises the various definitions adopted and the key findings from large-scale household surveys. Regardless of the definition used, the research has consistently found that young people are most likely to binge drink, particularly young men.

The nature of binge drinking

In addition to surveys measuring the extent of binge drinking, there has been a growth in qualitative research exploring the motivations for, and nature of, binge drinking.

Several authors (Casswell, 1993; Gilbert, 1990; Rehm, 1996) have stressed that the social dimension of alcohol is important. Studies have found that the amount drunk is linked to sociability. Nezlek et al., (1994) examined the relationship between a multidimensional measure of social interaction and binge drinking and found that those who reported some binge drinking had more intimate interactions. Observations of drinkers in licensed premises also found that drinking appeared to be heavier in groups, particularly same sex groups (Aitken, 1983). Following on from this, drinking seems to be heavier on popular group nights out; traditionally, in the UK, Friday and Saturday. Binge drinking is most often linked to drinking lager (Aitken, 1983; Moore, 1994) and practices such as circuit drinking – drinking in a succession of pubs in one evening – may increase the risk of binge drinking (Felson et al., 1997). MacAskill et al., (2001) through focus groups with young people aged 15 to 24 found that alcohol played a central role in the lives of those interviewed and was regarded as the main and sometimes the only leisure option.

Binge drinking, young people and crime

Although, there has been research into the extent and nature of binge drinking, relatively little research has been undertaken to explore the relationship between binge drinking and crime and disorder. Research into the association between alcohol and crime has often focused on the location and time of incidents, identifying the concentration of incidents on weekend nights in and around public houses, rather than examining binge drinking directly. The research that has been conducted is summarised briefly below.

Studies of student populations have examined the links between binge drinking and a range of social harms, including involvement in crime. Studies of students in the US and the UK have shown that high levels of binge drinking are associated with factors such as taking illicit drugs and involvement with the police (Marlatt, 1995; Webb, 1996; Wechsler, 2000). Wechsler (1995) found a link between binge drinking (5/4 or more drinks in a row) and students who experienced problems such as injury, committing vandalism and being involved with the police.

Studies of arrestees indicate that the majority of those arrested late at night in city centre areas are intoxicated with alcohol (Saunders, 1998; Deehan *et al.*, 2002). Deehan *et al.*, (2002) found that intoxicated arrestees were most often arrested for alcohol-specific offences (e.g. drunk and disorderly), public order offences or assault. Almost half of the intoxicated arrestees were aged between 18 and 24.

Studies carried out in Accident and Emergency settings have demonstrated that binge drinking is connected to increased risk of injury arising from an assault (Cherpitel, 1993; Shepherd and Brickley, 1996; Borges, 1998). Research carried out by Shepherd and Brickley (1996) in a large city centre A&E department compared males aged 18 to 35 attending with assault injuries with controls and found that consumption of more than ten units of alcohol in the six hours prior to assault was associated with injury.

Midanik (1999) using the US National Alcohol Surveys of 1979 and 1995 compared three measures of heavier drinking to examine which measures were most strongly related to a range of social harms. The analysis only included those who reported consuming alcohol in the past year. The social harms included involvement in heated arguments or fights, being questioned or warned by a police officer and being in trouble with the law. The results indicate that measures of drunkenness 'appear to predict social consequences, alcohol dependence symptoms and alcohol-related harm better than what appears to be the more objective 5+ measure' (p.895).

The physical and social context within which alcohol consumption takes place has been found to be a powerful indicator of alcohol-related problems. Homel *et al.*, (2001) outlined risk and protective factors for alcohol-related crime in licensed premises. The risk factors include high noise levels, inadequate seating, crowding, irresponsible server practice, inadequate door policy and poor bar cleanliness. As well as addressing these factors, other protective measures include encouraging eating with drinking, establishing protocols around pool tables, discouraging drinking to intoxication, fostering a positive social attitude and keeping out aggressive people.

Binge drinking and drug taking

Until recently there has been little research examining the relationship between binge drinking and illicit drug use. Recent studies have provided evidence that alcohol and illicit drugs do occupy the same arena. Measham (1996) found that 'heavier use of illicit drugs is linked with heavier use of alcohol' (p.294). Similarly, in studies of clubbers and young adults, drinking to the point of intoxication as well as taking illegal drugs was not uncommon (Parker *et al.*, 1998; Measham *et al.*, 2001). Parker *et al.*, 1998, suggested as well as illegal drugs and alcohol being deliberately used in combination, often to produce specific effects, the disinhibiting effects of alcohol sometimes lead to unplanned drug use.

This study

The research studies summarised in the previous section have often been based on relatively small or select samples (e.g. students, arrestees, those attending Accident and Emergency Departments). While they provide an indication that binge drinking is associated with offending behaviour, it is difficult to generalise from the results or to explore the extent of the link between binge drinking and crime and disorder.

The current study was designed to extend our knowledge about the extent and nature of the link between binge drinking and offending behaviour. It is primarily based on new secondary analysis of the 1998/1999 Youth Lifestyles Survey (YLS). The YLS, a large-scale, representative, household survey of 12- to 30-year-olds living in England and Wales, provides a unique opportunity to examine the relationship between patterns of alcohol consumption and offending behaviour. The survey was designed to measure the extent and nature of offending among young people and to examine the factors that may be associated with offending behaviour, including alcohol and drug use. This study focused on the links between binge drinking and offending behaviour among young adults aged 18 to 24 (i.e., the group found in previous research to be most likely to engage in binge drinking). In addition, 27 in-depth interviews were undertaken with young adults recruited from licensed premises in busy entertainment areas who reported drinking more than 8/6 units on a typical weekend night and feeling very drunk at least once in the past year to explore their perceptions, motivations and experiences of binge drinking. The qualitative interviews are not representative; they are based on a relatively small sample and cannot be generalised to the whole population. Nevertheless, they provide rich contextual data with which to explore the context and processes of binge drinking and offending behaviour. Further details of the methodology are provided in Appendix C.

2.   Patterns of drinking behaviour

This chapter provides an overview of the drinking behaviour of young people aged 18 to 24. It presents findings from the 1998/1999 Youth Lifestyles Survey on:

- the prevalence and frequency of alcohol consumption;
- the amount and type of alcohol consumed;
- experiences of intoxication;
- the social context within which alcohol is consumed; and
- perceptions as to why young people drink alcohol.

The chapter focuses on the 18- to 24-year-old age group but comparisons are made, where relevant, with those aged 25 to 30.

Prevalence of alcohol consumption

The vast majority of young people have consumed alcohol at some time. Ninety-seven per cent of those aged 18 to 24 said that they had drunk alcohol at least once in their lifetime, with 95 per cent having drunk alcohol in the twelve months prior to interview, and 78 per cent in the seven days prior to interview. While a similar proportion of men and women aged 18 to 24 had consumed alcohol at some time in the last year, men were significantly more likely to have consumed alcohol in the last seven days (Figure 2.1). Those aged 25 to 30 were significantly less likely to have drunk alcohol in the last seven days (Table A2.1).

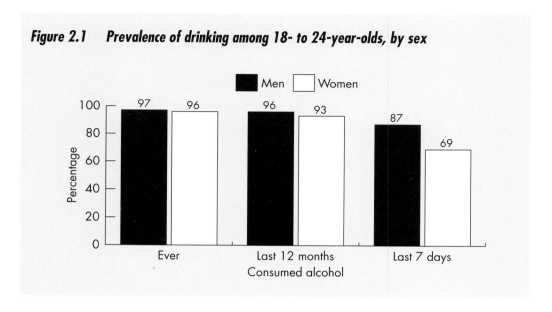

Figure 2.1   Prevalence of drinking among 18- to 24-year-olds, by sex

Frequency of alcohol consumption

Among those who had drunk alcohol in the preceding twelve months, the majority drank on a regular basis. One-tenth of 18- to 24-year-olds drank every day or nearly every day of the week, and a further two-thirds drank at least once a week. Around one in ten drank once or twice a month, with the remainder drinking less frequently. Young men were significantly more likely to admit drinking alcohol more than once a week than young women (see Figure 2.2). The pattern was generally very similar for those aged 25 to 30, though the older age group was somewhat less likely to drink more than once a week (Table A2.1).

Figure 2.2   Frequency of drinking among 18- to 24-year-olds who had drunk in the last year, by sex

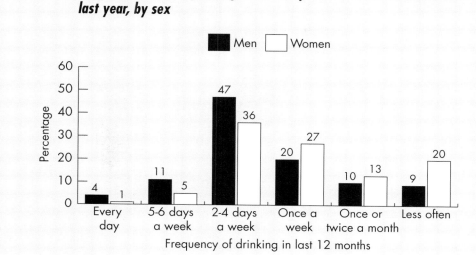

In terms of the prevalence and frequency of alcohol consumption, the YLS findings are generally consistent with those from other household surveys, such as the General Household Survey (GHS), Health Survey for England and the ONS Omnibus Survey module on adults' drinking behaviour and knowledge.

Type and amount of alcohol consumed

Young people who had drunk alcohol in the seven days prior to the interview (78% of all 18- to 24-year-olds) were asked about the types of alcoholic drink they had drunk during that time and the amount of each type of drink consumed.

Types of alcoholic drink consumed

Among 18- to 24-year-olds who had drunk alcohol in the previous week the most commonly consumed drink was beer or lager (79%), followed by spirits or liqueurs (55%) and wine (40%). There were differences in the drink preferences of men and women. Beer or lager was by far the most common drink among men, with 94 per cent saying they had drunk beer or lager in the previous week. The next most common drink type, spirits or liqueurs, had been drunk by 48 per cent. In comparison, young women were most likely to drink spirits or liqueurs (63%), closely followed by beer or lager (60%). Despite the much publicised launch of alcopops in the mid- 1990s, these drinks were less popular than beers, spirits or wine among 18- to 24-year-olds (Figure 2.3). Men and women aged 25 to 30 were significantly less likely to drink alcopops and spirits or liqueurs than their younger counterparts, and were significantly more likely to drink wine (Table A2.2)

Figure 2.3   Types of alcohol consumed among 18- to 24-year-olds, by sex

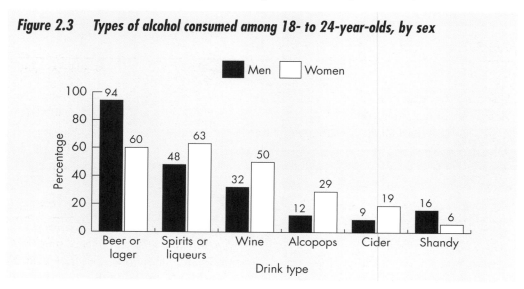

A quarter of 18- to 24-year-old drinkers had only consumed one type of alcoholic drink in the preceding week, with a further third having consumed two types of drink. However, a sizeable minority had drunk a relatively wide range of drinks, with 13 per cent drinking four or more types of alcohol (Table A2.2). Although women were slightly more likely to report drinking four or more alcohol types (15% vs 11%) the difference was not statistically significant. Among 25- to 30-year-olds, six per cent had consumed four or more drink types, with men being significantly more likely to do so than women (8% vs 3%).

Amount of alcohol consumed
Although measuring the frequency of alcohol consumption is difficult, measuring the amount of alcohol consumed is even more problematic. Not only is the accuracy of recall an issue but there are also difficulties in asking respondents to directly report the number of units of alcohol consumed over a given period. This is because both the definition is relatively complex and the process of calculating units based on number and type of drink consumed is a demanding exercise to undertake during an interview. Therefore, respondents were asked a series of questions to assess the number of various alcoholic drinks consumed in the previous seven days, in terms of standard measures, such as half a pint of beer or a glass of wine. Based on this data it was then possible to calculate the total number of units consumed using the unit definitions

shown in Box 2.1. This approach to measuring alcohol consumed is commonly used in surveys, though there remain measurement problems, not least because drinks vary in strength of alcohol content and drinks poured at home are likely to be larger than standard measures.

Box 2.1   *Unit content of standard drinks*

Drink type	Number of units
Half a pint, a bottle or a can of beer or lager	1 unit
Half a pint or a can of cider	1 unit
A glass of wine (including champagne and Babycham)	1 unit
A single measure of spirit or liqueur	1 unit
A bottle or can of alcoholic lemonade, alcopop or flavoured alcoholic drink	1.5 units
Half a pint or a can of shandy	1 unit
Half a pint, a bottle or can of other alcoholic drink	1 unit

In terms of weekly consumption, many in the health field recommend that women should drink no more than 14 units of alcohol a week and men should drink no more than 21 units of alcohol per week[8]. Among 18- to 24-year-olds who had drunk alcohol in the week prior to interview a sizeable minority had exceeded these limits (34% of men and 28% of women). Overall, among all 18- to 24-year-olds – 28 per cent of men and 19 per cent of women had drunk more alcohol in the week prior to interview than recommended (Table A2.3). The respective figures for 25- to 30- year-olds were significantly lower at 23 per cent and nine per cent. These results are similar to those found in other surveys which consistently indicate that 18- to 24-year-olds are most likely to exceed the weekly recommended limits (e.g. GHS, 2001).

Experiences of intoxication

While information on units of alcohol consumed is important in assessing patterns of alcohol consumption, particularly in terms of health outcomes, from a criminal justice perspective more subjective measures of intoxication are also useful. This is because the potential consequences of intoxication, such as heightened levels of aggression and impaired cognitive functioning, may be risk factors in experiences of crime and disorder, whether in relation to being a victim or perpetrator.

---

8.   This was the sensible drinking advice from the Department of Health until 1995. The current Department of Health advice relates to daily benchmarks of not more than 3-4 units of alcohol per day for men and not more than 2-3 units of alcohol per day for women.

The YLS asked respondents how frequently they had felt 'very drunk' and how frequently they had experienced a hangover in the previous twelve months. 18- to 24-year-olds were significantly more likely to admit to frequently experiencing drunkenness or hangovers than 25- to 30-year-olds. Among 18- to 24-year-olds who had drunk alcohol in the past twelve months, twelve per cent said they had felt 'very drunk' at least once a week. A further 29 per cent said they felt 'very drunk' at least once a month. Eight per cent reported having a hangover at least once a week, 18 per cent about 'once or twice a month'. Young men were significantly more likely to say they frequently felt 'very drunk' or have a hangover than young women (Figure 2.4, Table A2.4).

Figure 2.4 *Frequency of intoxication among 18- to 24-year-olds, by sex*

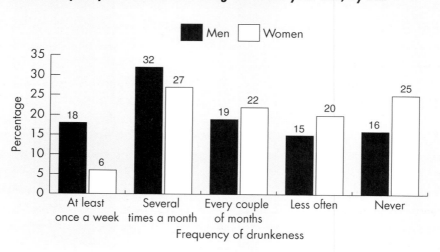

Social context of drinking

The YLS shows that the majority of young people aged from 18 to 24 drink alcohol frequently and a substantial minority drink excessively, either in terms of exceeding the weekly recommended unit limit or in terms of feeling 'very drunk' on a regular basis. However, it is important to extend the analysis to identify the social context in which young people consume alcohol and the reasons they choose to drink. While quantitative surveys are not best placed to examine these issues in-depth, the YLS data does provide some information.

Social context

The YLS found that the most common leisure activity among 18- to 24-year-olds, apart from watching the television, was going to a pub or going to a party, dance, nightclub or disco. Around eight in ten young people said they had been to a pub in the last month and three-quarters had been to a party, dance, nightclub or disco. Visiting venues where alcohol is available and an important part of the culture is therefore a central element in the lifestyles of young adults. Moreover, those who did consume alcohol usually did so in pubs or bars, rather than elsewhere. Seventy-nine per cent of 18- to 24-year-olds said they normally drank in a pub or bar; 35 per cent in a nightclub. Drinking alcohol was a social event, with the vast majority of 18- to 24-year-olds saying they usually drank with friends (87%). Forty-six per cent said they usually drank with a partner (husband/wife/partner/boyfriend/girlfriend).

The social context of drinking among those aged from 25 to 30 was somewhat different. While visiting pubs, bars and nightclubs remained a relatively common activity, it was far less so than among 18- to 24-year-olds. Similarly, although drinking in pubs or wine bars remained the most popular location for drinking (70%), this was closely followed by in the home (61%). Drinking was more likely to take place with partners (62%) and less likely to take place with friends (75%) than among the 18- to 24-year-old group. (Table A2.5).

Reasons for drinking

The YLS asked young people whether they agreed or disagreed with a series of six statements giving reasons why young people of their own age may drink alcohol. Those aged from 18 to 24 were most likely to agree with the two statements relating to the social context of drinking: 'young people drink to be sociable with their friends' (91%) and 'young people like going to pubs and clubs' (92%). However, three-quarters agreed that young people of their age drink because of the intoxicating effect of alcohol; 'they like getting drunk'. Figure 2.5 shows the results for men and women separately. Men were significantly more likely to agree that people their age drank to relax, to get drunk and because there was nothing else to do.

Those aged from 25 to 30 were far less likely to agree that people of their age drank because they liked getting drunk (51%) or because of boredom (17%). See Table A2.6.

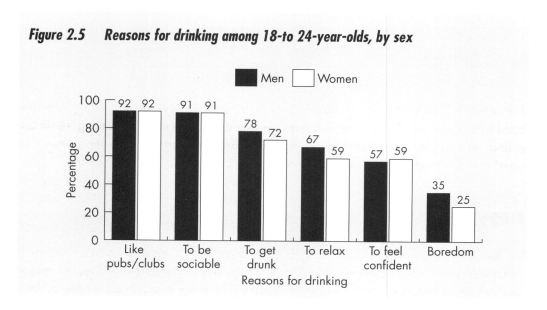

Figure 2.5   Reasons for drinking among 18-to 24-year-olds, by sex

Summary

This chapter has provided an overview of the drinking patterns of young adults based on analysis of the 1998/1999 Youth Lifestyles Survey. The results show that drinking alcohol is a very common and frequent activity for the majority of 18- to 24-year-olds, and forms an integral part of their lifestyles, particularly in relation to socialising with friends and visiting pubs, bars and night clubs. A substantial minority drink alcohol at levels that give cause for concern, either consuming more than the recommended weekly intake or experiencing intoxication on a frequent basis. Young women tend to drink less frequently than men and are less likely to drink to excess. These findings are consistent with the body of previous research, both qualitative and quantitative, that has examined young adults' experiences of alcohol.

3.   Binge drinking

The previous chapter described the drinking patterns of young adults, focusing on those aged from 18 to 24. This chapter discusses the extent of 'binge drinking' among 18- to 24-year-olds, examines the profile of young binge drinkers and explores the patterns of drinking they engage in. First though, the concept of 'binge drinking' is discussed.

Defining binge drinking

The term binge drinking has been widely used in recent years to describe a type of drinking behaviour which involves the consumption of a relatively large amount of alcohol over a relatively short period of time. The term has principally been associated with the drinking patterns of young people, in particular drinking in pubs, bars and clubs on a Friday or Saturday night. In turn binge drinking has been linked with the disorderly, and sometimes violent incidents, that occur in many town and city centres on Friday and Saturday nights. However, much of the research evidence on the links between binge drinking and disorderly behaviour is indirect (for example, studies identifying the concentration of violent and disorderly incidents in time and space) or based on relatively small or select samples (see Chapter 1).

Despite the common use of the term binge drinking there is no single standard definition that has been employed within the research community. Two broad types of definition have been used. The first is based on the units of alcohol consumed in a given period, with binge drinkers being those who have consumed more than a given number of units during the stated period. For example, drinking ten or more units in a single drinking session, drinking more than half the recommended number of units for a week in one drinking session. The second is based on self-reported experiences of intoxication, for example those who admit to feeling drunk on a regular basis, such as once a week.

While the former approach has the advantage of being based on a measure of alcohol consumed, it has been criticised because numerous factors, including personality, level of tolerance to alcohol, and the physical, social and cultural context, can all affect the impact that alcohol has upon an individual. In addition, unit definitions are usually based on questions that ask about alcohol consumed over a relatively short time period, often the last seven days, because of difficulties in respondents accurately recalling such information. For some individuals the last seven days may be atypical. The latter subjective approach addresses these problems by asking people to report how frequently they have felt intoxicated, over a longer period, for example a year. However, different people may well have different views as to what 'feeling drunk' entails.

YLS definition

The YLS offered the opportunity to examine both unit-based and intoxication-based definitions:

Unit-based definition – Men who had drunk more than eight units of alcohol on average per drinking day in the previous week were classified as binge drinkers, as were women who had drunk more than six units.

Intoxication-based definition – The second definition is based on self-reported frequency of having felt 'very drunk' in the last twelve months. Those who said they had felt very drunk 'once or twice a month', 'several times a month' or 'at least once a week' were classified as binge drinkers.

See Appendix C for further details.

The prevalence of binge drinking was far higher when using the intoxication definition. Almost four in ten (39%) 18- to 24-year-olds were classified as binge drinkers based on the intoxication definition[9], compared with a fifth based on the unit definition.[10] Among 25- to 30-year-olds the prevalence of binge drinking was significantly lower, the figures being 21 per cent and twelve per cent respectively. Figure 3.1 presents the results for men and women separately. Men were significantly more likely to be classified as binge drinkers regardless of definition, though the difference was more marked for frequent intoxication.

---

9.   Of those classified as binge drinkers on the intoxication definition, 29 per cent said they had felt 'very drunk' at least once a week, with the remainder admitting to being 'very drunk' at least once a month.
10.   Note that the prevalence of young people drinking above 6/8 units according to the YLS is lower than in the surveys presented in Appendix B. This is because the other surveys ask about heaviest drinking day in the week prior to interview, whereas the YLS figures are based on an average calculated from the total units consumed in a week divided by the number of drinking days.

Figure 3.1   Percentage classified as binge drinkers, by age and sex

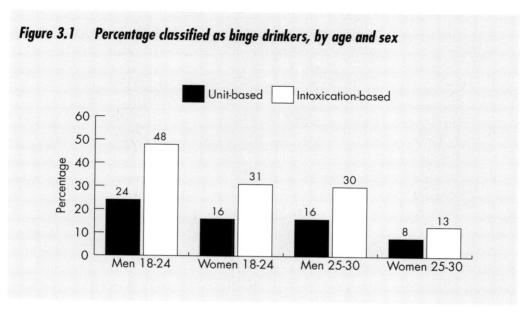

In terms of how the two definitions relate, thirteen per cent of all 18- to 24-year-olds were classified as binge drinkers according to both definitions, seven per cent were binge drinkers only in terms of units consumed, and 26 per cent only in terms of experiences of drunkenness in the last twelve months. Just over half (54%) were not classified as binge drinkers on either definition.

Analysis was undertaken using both definitions to explore the nature of binge drinking and the association with offending behaviour. The patterns were generally similar regardless of definition. The intoxication-based definition, however, is likely to be a more accurate measure of binge drinking, at least in part, because it is based on a regular pattern of binge drinking over a twelve month period, whereas the unit based definition is based on behaviour in the last seven days prior to interview, which may be atypical. Moreover, the unit-based definition will underestimate binge drinkers because it is based on average consumption across a week. For simplicity, only the intoxication-based definition is used throughout the remainder of this report.

In undertaking bivariate analyses, those who were not classified as binge drinkers were divided into those who regularly drank but did not regularly 'binge' (42% of 18- to 24-year-olds) and those who never or infrequently drank alcohol (18%). Figure 3.2 shows the drinking status profile of men and women age from 18 to 24 compared with those aged from 25 to 30.

The three-fold drinking classification enabled us to compare how regular binge drinkers differed from other regular drinkers who did not frequently drink to excess. In this chapter the focus is on these two groups though tables in Appendix A also present the results for the occasionally or never drinks group where possible.

Box 3.1   Drinking status groups

Binge drinkers	Those who reported feeling 'very drunk' at least once a month in the preceding twelve months.
Other regular drinkers	Those who have drunk alcohol at least once a month in the preceding twelve months, but say they have felt 'very drunk' less often than once a month.
Occasionally/never drinks	Those who have drunk alcohol less than once a month in the preceding twelve months, including those who had not drunk at all.

Figure 3.2   Drinking profile, by age and sex

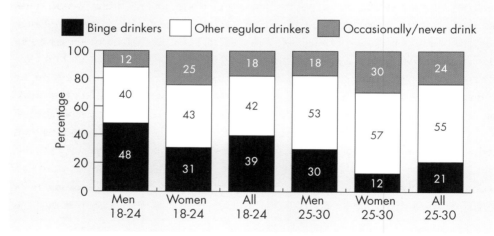

Socio-demographic profile of binge drinkers

In terms of their socio-demographic profile, binge drinkers did differ from other 18- to 24-year-olds who regularly drank. Binge drinkers were more likely to be male and single, and less likely to have children. Sixty-one per cent of binge drinkers were male, 92 per cent were single, and six per cent had children. The respective figures for those who regularly drank but did not regularly get drunk were 47, 82 and 13 per cent. The full results are presented in Table A3.1 in Appendix A.

Nature of binge drinking

Analysis was undertaken to explore how the drinking patterns of those classified as binge drinkers differed from other regular drinkers. Findings from the qualitative interviews with young people classified as 'binge drinkers' are also presented where relevant (see Appendix C for a discussion of the selection and interview process).

Frequency of drinking

According to the YLS, the vast majority of 18- to 24-year-old binge drinkers said they had drunk alcohol on at least a weekly basis during the past twelve months (Table A3.2). Ninety-five per cent reported drinking at least once a week, with almost a fifth admitting they had drunk alcohol almost every day of the week. The figures for other regular drinkers were significantly lower (78% and 5% respectively). Male binge drinkers were twice as likely to say they had drunk on every day or almost every day of the week than female binge drinkers (23% vs 11%) (Table A3.4).

The qualitative interviews also found that the majority of binge drinkers drank at least once a week. Almost all reported that they went out on either a Friday or Saturday night and more usually both nights. Respondents made a distinction between drinking at the weekend and during the week. Whilst weekday drinking was not uncommon, many felt that they moderated their drinking on weekday evenings in a way that they did not necessarily do on Friday and Saturday nights. The main reasons offered for this was the need to go to work the following morning. However, among students binge drinking tended to occur on 'student nights' during the week when alcohol was available more cheaply and heavy drinking was avoided when they had to complete college/university work the following day.

> *If I do go out in the week it would never be for much, a couple of drinks, because I'm working the next day or whatever*　　　　　　　　　　　　　　(Male, 21-24, southern city)

It was clear from the interviews that for many, weekend drinking brought different expectations than weekday drinking. The weekend was about meeting up with friends and escaping from the stresses of the working week. Alcohol played an important role in this process.

> *I work in [XXXX] and I'm not really happy in my job so I think it's one of them where you live for the weekend*　　　　　　　　　　　　　　(Female, 18-20, northern city)

Type and amount of alcohol drunk

The YLS found that among those who had consumed alcohol in the previous week, binge drinkers had consumed more types of alcoholic drink than other regular drinkers (Table A3.3). Around a fifth of binge drinkers had consumed four or more beverage types in the last seven days, compared with just under a tenth of other drinkers. Examining types of alcoholic beverage, binge drinkers were significantly more likely to report drinking beer and spirits or liqueurs than other regular drinkers. Among male binge drinkers the most popular drink was beer or lager, followed by spirits or liqueurs and wine. Among female binge drinkers spirits and liqueurs were most popular, followed by beer and wine (Table A3.4).

Although the YLS indicates that binge drinkers tend to drink a range of types of alcohol, it is unable to indicate the extent to which drinks are mixed during a single drinking session. The qualitative interviews addressed this issue and found that the majority of interviewees (all binge drinkers) mixed drinks during the course of an evening, particularly on weekend nights. Drinking often began in the home whilst getting ready for a night out, most usually wine, and often in the context of sharing with friends or housemates. Moving on to licensed premises, young adults discussed drinking several types of drink in one session as a way of becoming drunk more quickly. Alcopop type drinks were very popular and there were indications that males particularly were using alcopops to prolong drinking, consuming beer, lager and spirits at the beginning of the evening and then moving on to the palatable alcopops later on.

> *Beers first. But when you get light headed then we go on to spirits and alcopops and stuff* (Male, 18-20, southern market town)

Females were more likely to drink alcopops throughout the night, maybe in combination with spirits or shooters. New style shooter or chaser drinks (measures of sweetened, flavoured spirits often served in ready-made shot glasses and designed to be drunk in one go) were extremely popular.

The underlying message from the interviewees was that they wanted to feel drunk and deliberately moved between drink types as evenings progressed to aid this process. Drunkenness was considered to be an inevitable and desirable part of a 'big night out', although interviewees claimed that they rarely or never drank to the extent to which they felt 'out of control'. Interviewees often claimed that they knew their own limit through how they felt and were able to identify when they were at what they considered to be an acceptable or enjoyable level of drunkenness. Some said that friends intervened if they felt that someone had reached their 'limit'. What the 'limit' was for each individual, however, varied considerably and from discussions it proved that while many claimed they always remained 'in control' there were occasions when their behaviour was placing them in risky situations.

When you start to feel sick then I'll stop drinking then or when I'm told to stop drinking, then my mates will say 'that's it you've had enough now', that's when I'll stop
(Female, 21-24, northern city)

I hope I am quite sensible, I think so. I know when I am starting to get near my limits so I usually slow down
(Male, 21-24, southern market town)

I get drunk but not to the point where I am falling over and I don't [know] what I am doing – just to the point where you are merry and happy type of thing
(Female, 21-24, northern city)

Turning again to the quantitative data, the mean number of units consumed in the previous week was, not surprisingly, far higher among binge drinkers. The mean number of units consumed by those who were often drunk was 23.8, compared with 10.7 units for other regular drinkers (Table A3.3). Forty-two per cent of female binge drinkers who had drunk in the last week had consumed more than the recommended weekly limit, as had 48 per cent of male binge drinkers (Table A3.4).

Reasons for drinking

In terms of the reasons 18- to 24-year-olds gave for why young adults of their age drank alcohol the YLS found similarities between those classified as binge drinkers and other regular drinkers (Table A3.5). Both groups were most likely to agree with the social reasons (to be sociable and going to pubs/clubs), followed by 'to get drunk', and to feel relaxed and confident. However, binge drinkers were far more likely than other regular drinkers to agree that young people drank 'to get drunk' (86% compared with 68%) and somewhat more likely to say 'to relax', 'to feel confident' and because of 'boredom'. Male and female binge drinkers generally held very similar views as to why people their age drank alcohol (Table A3.6). However, male binge drinkers were significantly more likely to agree that young adults drank because 'they are bored and have nothing else to do' than their female counterparts. Conversely, female binge drinkers were more likely to cite 'confidence' than male binge drinkers.

The qualitative data supports the YLS findings. Social aspects of drinking (spending time with friends and meeting up with new people) were emphasised. Young people felt that alcohol assisted in the process through its disinhibiting qualities, allowing individuals to feel more confident and aiding social interaction (though as we see in Chapter 5 the disinhibiting impact was also considered to have a role in leading to criminal and disorderly incidents).

Alcohol was seen as important in heightening the enjoyment derived from a night out, through its impact on how the young people felt about themselves and the types of experiences they had when they had been drinking as opposed to when they were sober.

> *Yeah, it makes you a lot more confident. You go out and you chat to a lot more people than you would normally and a lot more women than you would normally as well*
> (Male, 18-20, southern market town)

> *I like that feeling of I don't care. I just want to dance. I shall have a good night. I'm happy and everything's bright. I'm giggly and people laugh at me because I'm funny and I love to make people laugh*
> (Female, 18-20, northern city)

Reiterating the point made above, another motivation for drinking alcohol was often as an escape from day-to-day problems, including work and relationships.

Interestingly, peer pressure was also mentioned by some interviewees as a factor that influenced their drinking behaviour. Young people often said they drank to fit in with the particular social group they were with at the time and their drinking behaviour was, to some extent, determined by whom they were with.

> *Because everyone else does it – which isn't really a reason but I'm not really going to go to a pub and sit there with a coke while everyone else is drinking alcohol and getting drunk*
> (Female, 18-20, southern city)

Social context

In terms of leisure activities in the month prior to interview, a similar proportion of binge drinkers and other regular drinkers had attended a pub, but binge drinkers were far more likely to report going to nightclub, dance or party. Ninety-one per cent of binge drinkers had attended a nightclub, dance or party, compared with 77 per cent of other regular drinkers. Binge drinkers were more likely to say they usually drank alcohol in a pub or bar or nightclub environment than other regular drinkers (Table A3.7). Eighty-eight per cent of binge drinkers usually drank in a pub or bar and 46 per cent in a nightclub. The figures for other regular drinkers were 79 per cent and 29 per cent respectively. Binge drinkers were also more likely to usually drink with friends and work colleagues than other drinkers. The usual drinking locations and companions of male and female binge drinkers were generally similar (Table A3.8).

Summary

This section has examined the drinking behaviour and attitudes of young people aged from18 to 24 who are classified as binge drinkers, compared with 18- to 24-year-olds who regularly drink but do not regularly binge. The findings indicate:

- Thirty-nine per cent of 18- to 24-year-olds frequently reported getting very drunk at least once a month and were classified as binge drinkers. Forty-two per cent were regular drinkers who did not regularly binge and a further 18 per cent only occasionally or never drank alcohol.
- Men were more likely to be classified as binge drinkers (48%) than young women (31%).
- Ninety-five per cent of binge drinkers consumed alcohol on at least a weekly basis, with around a fifth drinking almost daily. The qualitative interviews indicated that binge drinkers tended to binge drink on weekend nights and moderated their drinking during the week.
- Binge drinkers tended to drink a variety of alcoholic beverages. Around a fifth had drunk four or more types of alcohol in the week prior to interview. Compared with other drinkers, binge drinkers were more likely to consume beer and spirits and liqueurs. The qualitative interviews indicated that young adults deliberately mixed their drinks during the course of the evening in order to get drunk.
- Almost half of binge drinkers consumed in excess of the recommended weekly unit intake during the previous week.
- The most common reasons given for why young people drink were social, but among binge drinkers around nine in ten felt that young people drank 'to get drunk'.
- Binge drinkers said they normally drank in pubs/wine bars, followed by nightclubs, and most often drank in the company of friends.
- Compared with female binge drinkers, male binge drinkers were more likely to drink frequently, consume more units in a week, and agree that young people drank because they are 'bored'.

4.   Binge drinking and illicit drugs

There has, until recently, been relatively little research into the relationship between patterns of alcohol consumption and illicit drug use among young people and how both may be associated with criminal and disorderly behaviour. This chapter examines the prevalence of illicit drug use among young people and whether patterns of alcohol use are associated with patterns of illicit drug use. First, the findings from the Youth Lifestyles Survey are presented. This is followed by a discussion of the issues emerging from the in-depth interviews. Chapter 5 goes on to examine links with other offending behaviour.

YLS findings

The 1998/99 YLS asked respondents whether they had taken a variety of drugs ever in their lifetime and in the last year. This chapter focuses on drug use in the past twelve months. As in the previous chapter, patterns of drinking have been classified as follows:

- *binge drinkers* – those who reported getting very drunk at least once a month
- *other regular drinkers* – those who drank at least once a month but got drunk less than once a month
- *occasionally/never drink* – those who occasionally or never drank alcohol

We begin by examining whether drinking patterns are associated with illicit drug use, in particular whether binge drinkers are more likely to have taken illicit drugs. Then we explore, using the technique of logistic regression, whether drinking patterns remain associated with drug use even after other factors often linked to drug use are taken into account. It should be noted that the YLS does not allow us to explore the degree to which young adults may consume alcohol and illicit drugs in a single episode.

Prevalence of drug taking

Overall, four in ten 18- to 24-year-olds said that they had taken an illegal drug in the twelve months prior to interview. Young men were more likely than young women to admit taking drugs. Almost half of the men reported taking an illegal drug compared with just over a third of women. Drug use was significantly lower among the 25- to 30-year-olds, of whom a quarter had taken illegal drugs in the previous year (Figure 4.1).

Figure 4.1   Prevalence of drug taking among 18- to 30-year-olds, by sex

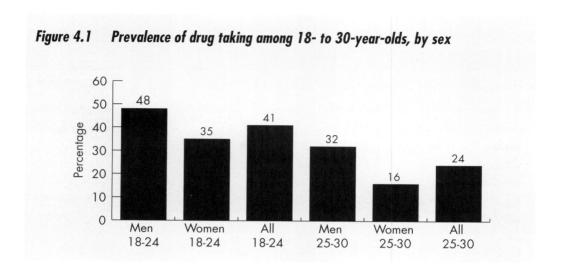

Those aged from 18 to 24 were significantly more likely to have used each type of illegal drug than the older age group. Among 18- to 24-year-olds men were significantly more likely to admit use than women. Cannabis was the most widely taken drug. Thirty-eight per cent of 18- to 24-year-olds had used cannabis in the past twelve months. Amphetamine was the next most popular drug, with seventeen per cent of 18- to 24-year-olds reporting they had used the drug. Around a tenth of 18- to 24-year-olds had taken ecstasy or cocaine, but less than one per cent said they had taken heroin or crack. (Table A4.1).

Binge drinking and drug taking

Turning to the relationship between drinking patterns and drug use, the YLS shows that among 18- to 24-year-olds frequency of drunkenness is strongly associated with illicit drug use. Overall, 59 per cent of binge drinkers reported taking illicit drugs in the previous year, compared with 33 per cent of those who drank regularly but did not binge. Binge drinkers were significantly more likely to have used most of the drugs asked about, with the exception of LSD and heroin. A quarter of those who drank less frequently or not at all said that they used an illegal drug (Table 4.1).

Table 4.1   Illicit drug use in the last 12 months among 18- to 24-year-olds, by binge drinking status

Percentages	Binge drinker	Other regular drinker	Occasionally/never drinks
Cannabis	55	30	21
Amphetamine	29	9	10
Ecstasy	16	6	5
Cocaine	15	6	1
Amyl nitrate	9	3	3
Magic mushrooms	8	2	1
LSD/acid	4	3	2
Crack	1	<1	0
Heroin	1	1	0
Any drug	59	33	24
Base N[2]	500	546	271

Notes:
1. Source: 1998/1999 Youth Lifestyles Survey.
2. The base number varied slightly for the different drug types – that shown is for the any drug category.

Almost two-thirds of male binge drinkers had taken an illegal drug in the past twelve months and were significantly more likely to admit use of all types of drugs asked about, with the exception of heroin and LSD, than males who regularly drank but not to excess. This pattern also held among young women, particularly for the most popular drugs. Females who reported being frequently drunk were around three times more likely to have taken amphetamines and ecstasy and almost twice as likely to have taken cocaine (Table A4.2).

The results of logistic regression

The analysis presented above indicates that young people aged from 18 to 24 who binge drink are more likely to consume illicit drugs than other young people aged from 18 to 24. However, many other socio-demographic and lifestyle factors have also been found to be related to drug use, such as educational achievement and income (see for example Ramsey et al., 2001). Multivariate analysis is required to isolate the independent influence of different factors. Logistic regression was therefore used to establish whether drinking behaviour, particularly binge drinking, was predictive of drug use among 18- to 24-year-olds once other relevant factors had been taken into account. Frequency of drinking and frequency of drunkenness were entered into the models to enable us to identify which was most strongly related to offending behaviour. Other independent variables were selected based on previous research. However, in interpreting the results it should be noted that some factors that may impact on drug use were not collected in the YLS. Models were tested for 'any drug' and for the most frequently consumed drugs: cannabis, amphetamine, cocaine and ecstasy.

Table 4.2 summarises the factors that were significantly predictive of drug use once other factors had been taken into account. The results clearly show that frequency of drunkenness remains strongly associated with drug use, both overall and for the four different drug types, even after other factors are taken into account. Overall, those who said they got very drunk at least once a week were about three and a half times as likely to have consumed illicit drugs in the previous twelve months than those who said they got very drunk less than once a month. The relationship was particularly strong for cocaine and amphetamine use. Interestingly, visiting a pub or club in the month prior to interview was highly predictive of cocaine use only. Recent research has particularly attributed the recent rise in the popularity of cocaine to use among affluent, young men who also drink a great deal of alcohol (Corkery, 2001; Ramsey et al., 2001; Pearson, 1998).

Frequency of drinking was less predictive of drug use than frequency of drunkenness. Drinking alcohol at least once a week was associated with cannabis use and overall drug use, but did not emerge as a factor for amphetamine, cocaine or ecstasy use.

Aside from frequency of drunkenness, the only other factors that were independently associated with the use of all four drugs were being male, being expelled or excluded from school and living in privately rented accommodation. Males were about one and a half times more likely to have taken drugs than females, holding all other factors constant, while those who had been excluded or expelled from school were about four times more likely to have taken drugs.

Table 4.2   Predictive factors for 18- to 24-year-olds – drug use

	Any Drug	Cannabis	Amphetamine	Cocaine	Ecstasy
Frequency of drinking (base: less than once a month)					
At least once a week	✓	✓	✗	✗	✗
Frequency of drunkenness (base: less than once a month)					
At least once a week	✓	✓	✓	✓	✓
Once or twice a month	✓	✓	✓	✓	✓
Visiting pub/club in last month	✗	✗	✗	✓	✗
Employment (base: working)					
Studying	✗	✗	✓-ve	✗	✓-ve
Unemployed	✗	✗	✗	✗	✓
Qualifications (base: higher)					
Other	✗	✗	✓	✓	✗
None	✗	✗	✗	✓	✗
GCSE	✗	✗	✓	✗	✗
A levels	✗	✗	✓	✓	✗
Housing tenure (base: owner occupier)					
Privately renting	✓	✓	✓	✓	✓
Other factors					
Male	✓	✓	✓	✓	✓
21-24	✗	✗	✗	✓	✗
Single	✗	✗	✗	✗	✓
No children	✗	✓	✗	✗	✗
White	✓	✗	✓	✗	✗
Expelled	✓	✓	✓	✓	✓

Notes:
1. Source: 1998/1999 Youth Lifestyles Survey.
2. The variable spending money was also tested in the model but did not come out in the model.
3. ✓ indicates factor significantly increased odds. ✓-ve indicates factor significantly decreased odds.
    ✗ indicates factor not in model or not significant.

Various other factors came into the different models though were not consistent across the drug types (Table 4.2). For example, being white was associated with amphetamine use even after other factors were taken into consideration, while being older (21 to 24) was associated with cocaine use.

Table A4.3 (Appendix A) presents fuller results including the exponential of the coefficients (Expβ) which indicate the change in odds of drug use.

Qualitative data

The in-depth interviews (all with binge drinkers) explored attitudes towards illicit drugs, whether individuals consumed drugs during 'a night out' and perceptions regarding the impact illicit drugs have on individuals relative to alcohol.

The majority of the young adults interviewed said they had taken an illegal substance at some time, and often did so as part of a night out, especially if this involved going to a club. Ecstasy and cocaine were more likely to be taken during the night out, whereas cannabis was more usually taken in the house after drinking to 'chill out'. No one reported taking heroin or crack cocaine.

Most of those who reported using drugs were aware that mixing illicit drugs and alcohol was potentially problematic. Mixing alcohol and ecstasy, in particular, was generally considered to be a bad thing, mainly as it was felt that this combination led to loss of control. However, drinking and taking cocaine appeared to be more acceptable among young adults. Among some of the participants there was a belief that cocaine negated the effects of alcohol and indeed some people reported using cocaine in order to be able to drink more.

> I used to take just the drugs and not drink which was ok and then the past couple of years I started to drink and take them at the same time and I found that to be a lethal combination (Female, 21-24, southern city)

> If I was really, really drunk and took some cocaine I'd probably feel sober and vice versa, if I tried to drink it wouldn't have any effect (Female, 18-20, southern market town)

> Some people do cocaine and drink as well. If you drink with cocaine it stops you from getting too drunk (Female, 21-24, northern city)

Generally, those interviewed were more likely to believe that alcohol had a greater influence on disorder in the night-time economy than any illicit drug. Interestingly, it was not only those who discussed taking drugs on a night out that found the presence of alcohol more of an indicator of disorder. Non-drug takers often reported feeling more comfortable and less intimidated in pubs or clubs that had more of a drug-taking culture than a binge drinking culture. Cocaine alone, out of all types of drugs discussed, was thought by some people to be a factor in increased aggression and this was often attributed to the links with alcohol consumption discussed above.

> *I mean I've never got into trouble doing drugs, drinking sometimes, you know it can get out of hand* (Female, 18-20, Southern market town)

> *I think alcohol is more associated with people getting aggressive. You are more likely to get trouble when you are out with people drinking than you are with drugs* (Female, 18-20, northern city)

> *When you go into the clubs and half of them are on drugs, I mean there's no trouble in there, but when you go into the pubs where everyone is drinking, there's trouble* (Female, 21-24, northern city)

> *I find that people who are taking cocaine they generally want to drink and I think that probably increases aggression* (Female, 21-24, northern city)

Although most illegal drugs were not linked to aggression there was some discussion about how the use of illicit drugs could result in feelings of paranoia and mental health problems. Some interviewees also commented that, despite the links with aggression, drinking alcohol was a more 'social experience' than taking illicit drugs.

> *The people that are like off their head on cocaine or ecstasy and you just think how are you still going … they are completely oblivious and they are just like stuck, completely glazed over* (Male, 21-24, northern city)

> *I think drinking is friendlier, cos you're all having a drink together and you're all having a laugh and that sociable thing, whereas having a tablet is not as sociable* (Female, 21-24, northern city)

Summary

The YLS indicates that almost four in ten 18- to 24-year-olds had taken an illegal drug in the twelve months before interview. Binge drinkers were far more likely to have taken an illegal drug (59%) than those who often drank but did not binge drink (33%). With the exception of heroin and LSD, those who often got drunk were significantly more likely to have used all of the drugs asked about in the survey than those who only occasionally got drunk.

Multivariate analysis confirmed that frequency of drunkenness was associated with the most commonly used drugs, particularly amphetamine and cocaine, even after other factors were taken into account. Only being male, being excluded or expelled from school and living in privately rented accommodation were also predictive in all four models.

The qualitative interviews allowed us to explore the relationship between alcohol and drug use in more depth. The majority of young adults interviewed had taken an illicit drug at some time in their lives and many reported combining alcohol and drugs, most often cocaine, during a night out. There was a widespread belief that alcohol was a far greater factor in violence and disorder in the night-time economy than illegal drugs, with the possible exception of cocaine.

Research into substance use by young adults verify these findings and has also found an increasing tendency for young people to combine the use of alcohol and drug use in a single occasion (Measham *et al.*, 2001).

5.

Binge drinking, crime and disorder

The previous chapter explored the links between alcohol use and illicit drug use among young adults. This chapter turns to the relationship between binge drinking and offending behaviour. It explores the extent to which young people offend and examines whether binge drinking is associated with involvement in various types of crime and disorder. The statistical findings from the Youth Lifestyles Survey are presented first, followed by the contextual data from the in-depth interviews.

Youth Lifestyles Survey

The YLS allows us to explore the links between drinking patterns and offending in two ways: examining the association with general offending; and links with committing disorderly and criminal behaviour during or after drinking (see Box 5.1 for further details)[11].

Box 5.1

General offending – respondents were asked if they had committed various different offences in the twelve months prior to interview. It is possible to examine which socio-demographic and lifestyles factors, including drinking behaviour, are associated with offending. In this chapter we focus on the following broad offence categories:

- *Violent crime (assaults, including those against family members, group fights and robbery)*
- *Criminal damage (criminal damage and arson)*
- *Theft (thefts of/from vehicles, shoplifting, pick-pocketing, burglary and other thefts)*
- *Any offence (comprising all of the above plus fraud and forgery and handling stolen goods)*

In addition, involvement in *fights* is examined separately, as this type of behaviour is often considered to be particularly associated with drinking behaviour. It should be noted that this approach examines the statistical association between regular binge drinking and offending and does not directly assess if alcohol had been consumed prior to the offences committed.

---

11. Note that the sample sizes for the analysis presented in this chapter differ slightly because of varying levels of missing information (refusal and don't know responses). Moreover, in looking at general offending there are fewer cases due to a split sample experiment (see Stratford and Roth, 1999 for further details).

Consequences of drinking – respondents who had drunk alcohol in the previous twelve months were directly asked if they had been involved in the following disorderly or criminal acts during or after drinking alcohol:

- A *heated argument*
- A *fight*
- *Criminal damage* (broken, damaged or destroyed something that belonged to someone else)
- *Theft* (taken something that belonged to someone else)

An *'any consequence'* variable was constructed which incorporated all of the categories shown above. As the questions asked specifically about acts committed during or after drinking it is more likely that alcohol, or the social context in which alcohol was consumed, had a part to play, though it can not be assumed that a direct causal relationship existed. Again it is possible to examine if there is an association between patterns of drinking and involvement in these behaviours.

The three-fold drinking typology[12] was again used to allow us to examine whether regularly drinking to excess was more strongly associated with disorderly and criminal behaviour than frequent drinking per se. In addition, illicit drug use was considered in combination with alcohol use to examine to what extent different patterns of alcohol and drug use were linked with offending behaviour. Mulitivariate analysis was undertaken to examine if patterns of drinking emerged as significantly related to criminal and disorderly behaviour once other factors known to be associated with offending, including drug use, were taken into account.

General offending

Overall, a quarter of all 18- to 24-year-olds reported committing at least one of the offences asked about in the previous twelve months. Young men were significantly more likely to admit offending than young women (33% compared with 13%). Among young men violence was the most common offence (15%), followed by theft (12%). Among young women, theft was the most common offence type (4%). Those aged from 25 to 30 were far less likely to admit offending in the last year (Table A5.1).

Examining the association between drinking patterns and offending behaviour, binge drinkers aged from 18 to 24 years were almost three times more likely to admit to committing an offence than 18- to 24-year-olds who often drank but were infrequently drunk. For all offence groups binge drinkers were significantly more likely to admit to an offence. The difference was

---

12.   Binge drinkers; other regular drinkers and occasional or never drinkers (see Chapter 3 for details).

particularly marked for fights, with binge drinkers being five times as likely to admit to an incident (Figure 5.1). The prevalence of offending was lowest among 18- to 24-year-olds who occasionally or never drank alcohol – only eight per cent reported offending (Table A5.2).

Figure 5.1   Offending among 18- to 24-year-olds by binge drinking

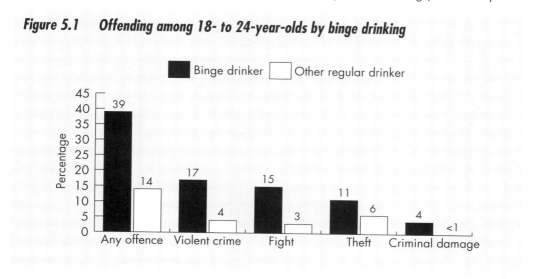

Offending behaviour was most prevalent among 18- to 24-year-old male binge drinkers. This held for all offence groups examined (Table A5.3). A quarter of binge drinking males reported being involved in violent crime compared with less than ten per cent of young men who often drank but were rarely drunk. These findings indicate that for young men frequency of drunkenness is more strongly associated with offending than frequency of drinking. For young women the relationship between frequency of drunkenness and offending was significant only for overall offending. There was no significant relationship between drunkenness and offending in any of the specified offence categories.

General offending, binge drinking and drug use

Binge drinking is clearly associated with offending behaviour. However, as established in the previous chapter drinking patterns are also strongly related to illicit drug use, which in turn is linked to offending behaviour. We therefore examined how different broad patterns of alcohol and illicit drug use in the last year were related to offending behaviour (Table 5.1).[13] Overall, 18- to 24-year-olds who were classified as binge drinkers and also reported drug use in the previous twelve months were most likely to report being involved in any

---

13.   A four-fold typology was developed based on whether classified as a binge drinker or not and whether used any illicit drug in the previous twelve months or not. Due to the relatively small number of individuals admitting use of particular drugs it was not possible to examine in more detail different patterns of drug use.

offending behaviour. Around a half (49%) did so. The prevalence of offending was slightly higher among those who had only taken drugs (28%) than those who only binged (23%) although this was not significant. However, the patterns did differ somewhat across the individual offence types. For example, those who only binged were more than twice as likely to admit a violent offence than those who only used drugs, while the opposite held for theft offences (the difference was not significant in the case of theft offences).

Table 5.1   *Offending in the last 12 months among 18- to 24-year-olds, by binge drinking and drug use*

Percentages	Drugs and binge	Drugs not binge	Binge not drugs	Not binge not drugs
Any offence in last twelve months	49	28	23	6
Violent Crime	19	6	13	2
Taken part in a group fight in public place	17	5	12	2
Theft	14	14	7	2
Criminal Damage	6	1	1	>1
Base N	204	150	146	406

Notes:
1. Source: 1998/1999 Youth Lifestyles Survey
2. Drugs – any drug use in the last twelve months. Binge – those reporting getting drunk at least once a month. Not binge includes other regular drinkers and occasional/never drinkers.

The results of logistic regression

The results presented in the preceding section indicate a significant relationship between binge drinking and offending behaviour, particularly among young men. Moreover, patterns of binge drinking and illicit drug use are related in different ways to different types of offence. Logistic regression was undertaken to establish if binge drinking remained predictive of involvement in offending among 18- to 24-year-olds taking into account various other factors associated with criminal and disorderly behaviour (see for example Flood-Page *et al.*, 2000), although it should again be noted that not all factors relating to offending behaviour were collected in the YLS. Frequency of drinking, frequency of drunkenness and drug use were each entered into the models to enable us to identify which was most strongly related to offending behaviour. Other independent variables were selected based on previous research. Table 5.2 summarises the factors that were significantly predictive of involvement in any offence, violent crime, fights and theft[14] (the full results are in Table A5.4).

---

14.   Criminal damage was not examined separately because the number of respondents admitting to the offence was very low.

Frequency of drunkenness was strongly associated with overall offending behaviour even after taking other factors into account, while frequency of drinking was not associated with offending behaviour. Examining the different offence groups, frequency of drunkenness increased an individual's odds of being involved in violent offending, but not theft. Those who said they had felt very drunk at least once a week were more than five times as likely to be a violent offender than those who said they were never drunk or drunk less than once a month. Those who said they were very drunk once or twice a month were three times as likely to commit a violent offence. Conversely illicit drug use was associated with an increased risk of theft, but was not related to violent offending. These findings reinforce the common perception that illicit drug use is associated with acquisitive crime, while alcohol use is associated with violent crime.

Other factors that were independently related to offending were as follows:
Being male – controlling for other factors, being male was significantly associated with having committed a theft and, in particular, a violent offence.
Delinquent acquaintances – knowing a person, whether it be a friend, family member or acquaintance, who had been involved in offending was significantly predictive of offending in all categories.
Being expelled or excluded – disrupted schooling through exclusion or being expelled was only associated with violent crime.

Table 5.2   *Offending in the last 12 months – predictive factors for 18- to -24-year-olds*

	Any offence	Violent crime	Fighting	Theft
Frequency of drunkenness (base: less than once a month)				
At least once a week	✓	✓	✓	✗
Once or twice a month	✓	✓	✓	✗
Other factors				
Male	✓	✓	✓	✓
Delinquent acquaintance(s)	✓	✓	✓	✓
Has been expelled/excluded from school	✗	✓	✗	✗
Used any drug in the last twelve months	✓	✗	✗	✓

Notes:
1. Source: 1998/1999 Youth Lifestyles Survey.
2. Employment status, ethnicity, children, marital status, educational qualifications, amount of spending money, frequency of drinking and going to pubs or clubs were also tested in the model but did not come out in the model.
3. ✓ indicates factor significantly increased odds. ✗ indicates factor not in model or not significant.

Consequences of drinking

The previous section demonstrated that binge drinking was significantly associated with general offending, even after other factors were taken into account. In this section we focus on criminal and disorderly behaviour that occurs during or after drinking, again examining how patterns of drinking behaviour are associated with such behaviour.[15]

Overall, 38 per cent of 18- to 24-year-old drinkers said that they had committed at least one of the four acts asked about in the previous twelve months (Table A5.5). Becoming involved in a heated argument was the most common experience, followed by involvement in a fight, breaking something and taking something.[16] The pattern was the same for men and women, though for each behaviour, men were significantly more likely to admit to an incident (Figure 5.2). Almost a quarter of young men reported having been in a fight compared with five per cent of young women. Twenty-five to 30-year-old drinkers were far less likely to admit becoming disorderly following drinking (Table A5.5).

Figure 5.2   Consequences of drinking among 18- to 24-year-olds by sex

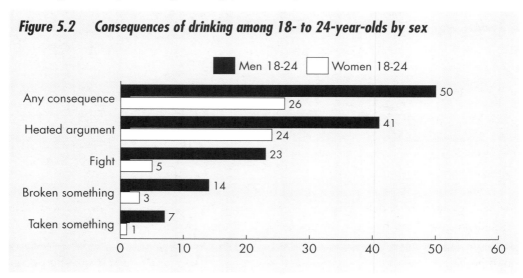

---

15.   Note that because the questions were about committing criminal and disorderly acts during or after drinking during the last twelve months only those who had drunk alcohol in the last twelve months were asked.

16.   Interestingly, the percentage admitting fighting and criminal damage during or after drinking is higher than when responding to general offending (fights and criminal damage) in the last year. While it is not possible to identify with certainty why this is there are several possible reasons. The two sets of questions are worded differently and in different sections of the questionnaire. Respondents may feel more comfortable admitting to such behaviour if they can excuse themselves through their drunken state or may feel that their behaviour while drunk did not really constitute a 'crime' thus failing to report to the 'general offending' set of questions. Moreover, reference to drinking in the question may prompt them to remember specific incidents which they failed to recall at the general questions.

Patterns of drinking were strongly associated with the likelihood of involvement in crime and disorder during or after drinking. Those 18- to 24-year-olds who were classified as binge drinkers were significantly more likely to admit to each of the four behaviours than other regular drinkers of the same age. Binge drinkers were more than twice as likely to participate in arguments during or after drinking, four times as likely to admit taking part in a fight, five times as likely to admit to criminal damage and eight times as likely to admit to a theft (Figure 5.3). Overall, 60 per cent of binge drinkers had committed at least one of the four behaviours, compared with 25 per cent of other regular drinkers and just over ten per cent of occasional drinkers (Table A5.6).

Figure 5.3   *Consequences among 18- to 24-year-olds by binge drinking*

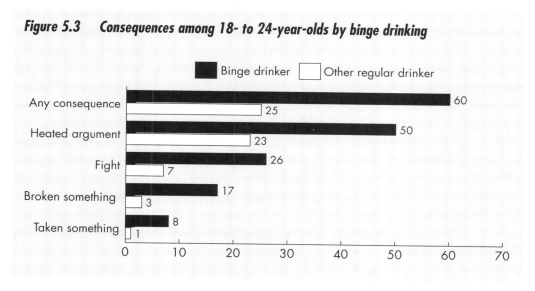

As with general offending, male binge drinkers were significantly more likely to have committed any of the behaviours than female binge drinkers (69% vs. 45%) (Table A5.7). Just over half of male binge drinkers had been involved in a heated argument, around a third had been involved in a fight, a quarter had damaged property and a tenth had stolen property.

Among women the link between patterns of drinking and disorderly behaviour during or after drinking was stronger than that found for general offending. In all categories, apart from taking something, female binge drinkers were significantly more likely to have committed the act than females who drank regularly but not to excess. This is perhaps not surprising as the 'consequences' questions provide a measure of alcohol-related offending.

Consequences of drinking, binge drinking and drug use

Turning to binge drinking and taking illicit drugs, 18- to 24-year-olds who reported both binge drinking and drug use were the most likely to admit to all of the criminal and disorderly acts during or after drinking alcohol (Table 5.3). Unlike in general offending, those who binge drank only were significantly more likely to admit to any of the behaviours than those who took drugs only (49% vs 34%). However, for individual offence types the difference was only significant for getting involved in a heated argument.

Table 5.3   Consequences in the last 12 months among 18- to 24-year-olds, by binge drinking and drug use

Percentages	Drugs and binge	Drugs not binge	Binge not drugs	Not binge not drugs
In the past 12 months has during or after drinking …				
…got into a heated argument	56	31	41	15
…got into a fight	31	12	17	4
…broken, destroyed or damaged something belonging to someone else	23	6	7	2
…taken something belonging to someone else	11	1	4	1
…done any of the above	66	34	49	17
Base N (those who had drunk last 12 mths)	288	210	212	529

Notes:
1. Source: 1998/1999 Youth Lifestyles Survey
2. Drugs – any drug use in the last twelve months. Binge – those reporting getting drunk at least once a month. Not binge includes other regular drinkers and occasional drinkers.

The results of logistic regression

The findings presented above indicate that among 18- to 24-year-olds, there is a link between binge drinking and committing disorderly or criminal acts during or after drinking alcohol. Again, the statistical technique of logistic regression was used to try and isolate the importance of drinking behaviour on offending whilst taking into account the other socio-demographic and lifestyles factors, including illicit drug use. Table 5.4 summarises the final models in predicting involvement in disorderly and criminal behaviour after drinking (full results are in Table A5.8).[17]

---

17. Taken something was not examined separately because the number of respondents admitting to the offence was very low.

As with the general offending models presented above, frequency of drunkenness remained strongly associated with criminal and disorderly behaviour during or after drinking even after other factors had been controlled for. Young adults who got very drunk at least once a week were almost seven times as likely to admit to criminal damage, five times as likely to admit to fighting and four times as likely to become involved in an argument than those who got drunk less than once a month. Those who said they got drunk once or twice a month were around three times as likely to be involved in any of these behaviours, compared with those who got drunk less often.

The only other factors that were predictive of involvement in all behaviours were being male and using illicit drugs in the previous twelve months.

Other factors that were independently related to committing a disorderly or criminal act after or during drinking were as follows:

Frequency of drinking – this was associated with the 'any consequences' category, with those who drank at least once a week doubling their risk of being involved in at least one of the specified behaviours, but not with the three individual behaviours examined.

Age of first drink – those who started to drink alcohol at a younger age were more likely to have been involved in heated arguments.

Age – this was associated with fighting only. An 18- to 20-year-old had more than double the odds of getting into a fight than a 21- to 24-year-old.

Qualifications – was also associated with fighting only. Those with no or unspecified qualifications were more likely to be involved in a fight.

Table 5.4   Consequences of drinking – predictive factors for 18- to 24-year-olds

	Any consequence	Heated argument	Got into a fight	Broken, damaged
Frequency of drinking (base: less than once a month)				
At least once a week	✓	✗	✗	✗
Frequency of drunkenness (base: less than once a month)				
At least once a week	✓	✓	✓	✓
Once or twice a month	✓	✓	✓	✓
Qualifications (base: degree/higher)				
Other – unspecified	✗	✗	✓	✗
None	✗	✗	✓	✗
Age of first drink (base: 15 to 24)				
1-12	✓	✓	✗	✗
13-14	✓	✓	✗	✗
Other factors				
Male	✓	✓	✓	✓
18-20	✗	✗	✓	✗
Used a drug in last twelve months	✓	✓	✓	✓

Notes:
1. Source: 1998/1999 Youth Lifestyles Survey.
2. Employment status, ethnicity, children, marital status, going to a pub or club and going out in the evening were also tested in the model but did not come out in the model.
3. ✓ indicates factor significantly increased odds. ✗ indicates factor not in model or not significant.
4. The 'other – unspecified' category includes all qualifications mentioned by respondents that did not fit in one of the qualification categories listed (for further details see Stratford and Roth (1999)).

Qualitative data

The statistical findings from the YLS show a strong and enduring relationship between drinking to intoxication and being involved in crime and disorder. It is impossible to conclude from this that excessive alcohol consumption is causally related to offending behaviour. However, the qualitative data allows us to explore young binge drinkers' experiences and perceptions of alcohol and criminal behaviour more closely. This section first looks at risky behaviour and crime and disorder during or after drinking, and then moves on to discuss the perceived behavioural effects of alcohol. Finally, issues surrounding the identification of 'problem groups' associated with drunk and disorderly behaviour are discussed. It must be stressed that the data presented are the views of the young adults interviewed and should not be considered representative of all 18- to 24-year-olds.

Criminal and disorderly behaviour

Among interviewees drinking an excessive amount of alcohol rarely led to criminal or disorderly activity (or certainly the admittance of such behaviour). However, the vast majority gave examples of times that they had done something they regretted, or felt they had put themselves in a risky situation under the influence of alcohol. In many cases interviewees had behaved in a way which increased their vulnerability to criminal victimisation.

I've got lifts with people that I don't know very well, got in cars with people who are drunk driving
(Female 21-24, southern city)

I think risks where I'd end up somewhere and I wouldn't have enough money to get home and it would be like I'm in the middle of nowhere, I don't know where I am, I'm going to have to get home
(Female, 18-20, southern city)

I've done really stupid things like get into cars with friends who are really, really drunk and I shouldn't have done. I've been in a car crash with my friend driving and she was really drunk
(Female, 18-20, northern city)

Some guy came up to me and he's talking and it's like talking to a normal guy and he's like could I borrow your phone? And I said yeah, no problem and he just ran off with it, he didn't even nick it, I just let him have it, but obviously that would have never happened if I'd been sober
(Male, 21-24, southern city)

A minority, however, had directly been involved in some sort of fight or assault whilst on a night out, whether as victim or perpetrator. Of the rest all had witnessed some form of crime and disorder, most commonly fights, including some relatively serious incidents involving 'glassings' or 'bottlings'.

I was walking past a girl who was very, very drunk and we just kind of bumped into each other and it started into an argument and me and my friend were just about to get into a cab but she came after me and hit me and then it went into a fight, the police came and everything
(Female, 18-20, southern city)

Just out of the blue, I was walking across by the bar and two guys touched shoulders and just went into each other, didn't even talk and the next thing they were on the floor
(Male, 18-20, southern city)

Some bloke staggered out, his face had been slashed with blood gushing out, police everywhere, he'd been bottled and that was only next door to the place I was in
(Male, 21-24, northern city)

I think you get a few stabbings but that's like broken bottles and blokes mostly cos I don't know any girls that have ever bottled someone but most blokes would, like if they got into a fight they'd pick up a bottle (Female, 18-20, southern city)

A couple of times when a lot of my friends actually got bottles smashed over their head when people would come out of the army barracks just drink like crazy and then look for a fight (Female, 21-24, southern city)

In most cases the person interviewed believed that alcohol had played a part in either starting or exacerbating the assault they witnessed or were involved in. Although there was also the perception that the people who initiated fights were people who went out looking for a fight, with alcohol serving to fuel that desire.

You do get the certain kinds who like a bit of a fight anyway, especially when they've got a few drinks into them, you know that kind of looking for it
(Female, 21-24, northern city)

I think for a lot of people that's their main reason for going out, to have some excitement either way, whether they start a fight or have a dance they want something to happen (Male, 21-24, northern city)

Effects of alcohol

Most of the people interviewed thought that alcohol had some sort of an effect on their own feelings and behaviour. A lot of interviewees spoke about different levels of drinking and changes in mood that occurred as they progressed through the different stages of drunkenness.

I get to a point where it puts you in a very good mood, it makes you feel relaxed, you're enjoying yourself but if I go beyond that point that's where the trouble starts
(Male, 18-20, southern market town)

My favourite kind of drunk is what a few of my friends call spangled, which is you're kind of like, you're past tipsy and your past merry but you're not into drunk
(Female, 21-24, northern city)

Often the effects of alcohol were described in terms of the effect it had on other people's behaviour. There was a general perception that alcohol clouded judgement and enhanced feelings of invulnerability, often leading to confrontation.

> It is a confidence thing because when you are drunk you think you can take on the world and I think anybody will start when they are drunk but when you are not drunk you have got a different perception to how you see people
>
> (Female, 18-20, southern city)

> It changes the way you think, it turns people, I don't know, much more argumentative, more arrogant, probably more full of themselves and they think they are it, so they think they can start on everyone and anyone
>
> (Female, 18-20, southern market town)

> It fuels people's desire to fight I suppose, it knocks out the constraints they would normally put on themselves when they are sober   (Male, 21-24, northern city)

In the young adults' experience when confrontation did occur it often led to physical aggression. Alcohol was perceived to act as a catalyst through its impact on behaviour and feelings of confidence and aggression. Interviewees also mentioned incidents that tended to trigger fights including, someone looking at (or perceived to be looking at) someone else's girlfriend, accidentally or carelessly pushing or bumping into someone, looking at (or perceived to be looking at) someone 'the wrong way', arguments or rivalries about football, and taking exception to someone's appearance.

> Looking at someone the wrong way, you see people in the pub, someone's knocked them, someone's talked to someone's girlfriend, things like that start it off
>
> (Female, 21-24, northern city)

> Staring at each other or staring at their girlfriends, or knocking their pint over or if there's a match on it will be about football   (Female, 21-24, northern city)

> Pissed people normally, getting too rowdy. If they bump into someone or something like that and he says, 'oy', and it just starts like that normally
>
> (Male, 18-20, southern market town)

Problem groups

There was also a feeling that the effect of alcohol and alcohol-related aggression was more pronounced in certain groups. Most commonly men, and particularly young men, were mentioned as being more likely to react aggressively after drinking. The masculine culture and the need to defend their image in front of friends and girlfriends was thought to be the basis for this.

It's like a big macho thing I guess, showing off in front of their mates and they're drunk which just makes them show off more   (Female, 18-20, northern city)

A lot of guys' testosterone levels start going up, you know the macho thing, squaring up and all that stuff   (Male, 18-20, southern market town)

Another group that was singled out for having a particularly adverse reaction to alcohol was under-age or younger drinkers. There was a perception that this group had not learnt to drink 'properly', were unable to judge their limits, and were therefore more likely to become very drunk and cause problems.

It's always the younger drinkers, they don't know their own personal reactions to certain types of alcohol but they'll just drink anything and they want all the strongest stuff   (Female, 21-24, southern city)

Summary

The YLS indicates that there is a strong relationship between patterns of drinking and offending behaviour, with frequency of drunkenness being strongly associated with both general offending behaviour and, more specifically, committing disorderly and criminal behaviour after drinking alcohol. Almost four in ten 18- to 24-year-old binge drinkers had committed at least one offence in the previous twelve months and six in ten had committed a disorderly or criminal act during or after drinking alcohol. The figures were significantly lower among those who drank regularly but not to excess (14% and 25% respectively). These results demonstrate that binge drinkers are more likely to be involved in criminal and disorderly behaviour. Moreover, the relationship between drunkenness and offending remained strong even after other socio-demographic and lifestyles factors associated with offending behaviour were taken into account. Multivariate analysis demonstrated that frequency of drunkenness was the factor most predictive of involvement in disorderly and criminal behaviour after drinking and far more predictive of general offending, with the exception of theft, than many other factors. Indeed, the only factor that was as strongly predictive of general offending was being male.

These results confirm that it is important to consider patterns of drinking when examining the links with crime and disorder. Regular binge drinking is far more strongly associated with offending behaviour than regular drinking per se. Although multivariate analysis goes some way to suggesting that binge drinking is directly related to offending behaviour, it does not necessarily follow that excessive alcohol is causally linked to offending. It is unlikely that the pharmacological effects of alcohol alone result in offending behaviour and more likely that an array of factors related both to the individual and the social environment in which they drink influence the likelihood of offending. The YLS data do not provide detailed information about incidents of offending to allow us to identify how incidents arise during or after drinking. However, the qualitative data provide some contextual information about how young people view the link between their alcohol consumption and offending and how various social and contextual factors impact upon this.

6.   Reducing alcohol-related crime and disorder

This chapter presents findings from the in-depth interviews. It focuses on the ideas that the young adults suggested as potentially being effective in tackling alcohol-related crime and disorder. Whilst it must be remembered that these views are not representative of the young adult population as a whole they do provide valuable insight into what young people think might work. Suggestions fell into two broad approaches: reducing drinking and tackling the associated crime and disorder. There were generally mixed views about whether the amount young people drink and alcohol-related crime could actually be reduced. There were also differing opinions about effective measures to reduce binge drinking and associated harmful consequences. However, a lot of interesting and innovative ideas were discussed.

Reducing drinking

Many of the interviewees were sceptical about the possibility of reducing the amount of alcohol the young adult age group consumed.

> *I think the only way you eradicate those kind of problems is to limit people on their drinking and you can't do that, that's not socially acceptable*
>
> (Female, 21-24, southern city)

> *If someone wants to drink they'll go on drinking no matter what people say unless they get a scare themselves or something happens to them*
>
> (Female, 21-24, southern city)

However, some thought there could be ways of encouraging more moderate consumption. Broadly suggestions fell into three categories; licensed premises, advertising, and education. Each of these is discussed further below.

Licensed premises

Many suggestions centred around licensed premises and what could be done within them to discourage excessive drinking and promote more moderate drinking. Some of the measures discussed may be the responsibility of the licensed trade rather than individual licensees.

Popular ideas were better server training so that bar staff took responsibility for controlling customers' drinking if deemed necessary, and promoting soft drinks and safe drinking messages within licensed premises. Placing safer drinking advice and unit content on bottles of alcohol was particularly considered to be a good idea. However, there was concern that some young drinkers would use unit information to select the strongest drinks therefore increasing consumption. Diverting people away from drinking or restricting drinks through standard limits on the amount any individual consumed were also mentioned as ways of reducing consumption.

I think sometimes the barmen don't notice when people are too drunk and they'll let them carry on because they want the money but I think the bar people should say you've had enough or you will get chucked out but they don't normally do that
(Female, 18-20, southern city)

It should be mandatory that pubs serve non-alcoholic drinks really cheaply to encourage people not to drink because you feel like you are being cheated
(Female, 21-24, southern city)

You could develop some system like a personal drinking card system or something like that which restricts people to a certain number of drinks per club
(Male, 18-20, southern market town)

I'd say the best way to encourage people to drink less is to offer as much as you can entertainment wise
(Female, 21-24, northern city)

Many of the young adults reported that they personally drank more than they usually would or drank different types of drinks during drink promotions or happy hours to take advantage of the reduced prices. Interestingly, none of those interviewed actually suggested banning 'happy hours', though given their own behaviour this would appear to be an approach that could reduce binge drinking.

Advertising

The use of alcohol advertising was discussed in the interviews. There were very mixed views about whether advertising, either sponsored by the government, brewing industry or other agency, was effective in communicating safe drinking messages thus reducing consumption levels. Most people could not recall seeing any information relating to safe drinking and if they had they were unsure as to exactly what message was being relayed. Most interviewees felt that for any message to be effective it had to be hard hitting and contain graphic images and most thought that television would be the most effective medium to achieve this. However, there was some belief that eye-catching posters would also be effective, especially if they were positioned carefully. Some suggested sites included pub toilets, alcohol aisles in supermarkets, and public transport. Encouragingly, nearly all of those interviewed mentioned the government's drink-drive campaign as being successful in impacting on people's attitudes and behaviours.

If I saw a poster in a bar, it wouldn't stop me having a drink you know, I wouldn't say ooh look at that, I've got to slow down, it wouldn't affect me

(Male, 21-24, southern city)

Posters you'll see one and think, oh god, I did something stupid like that when I was drunk so I think posters are quite effective. But I don't think they would make you go out a night and think I'll drink less because of what that poster said

(Female, 18-20, northern city)

Education

A popular view among interviewees was that there should be more alcohol education in schools and at quite an early age, though few were able to articulate the type of messages that should be promoted. Many mentioned that they remembered receiving drugs education at school but not alcohol education, or if they did it was to a far lesser extent than drugs education. The fact that the vast majority of interviewees seemed to know more about illegal drugs than alcohol (few knew about recommended drinking guidelines or the relative strength of drinks) seems to suggest that education might be effective in increasing knowledge.

Definitely the schools I have been to have put more of an emphasis on drugs, like drugs are bad they ruin your life, but with drink it is more like, well your parents drink just don't become an alcoholic (Male, 18-20, southern market town)

They do drug related classes now in primary schools, they should probably incorporate drinking into that (Female, 21-24, southern city)

Reducing crime and disorder

As well as measures that could be taken to reduce alcohol consumption, the interviewees talked about how the harm related to drunkenness could be minimised. Three areas in particular will be discussed: policing, licensed premises, and city planning.

Policing

The majority of interviewees felt that a large and visible police presence in areas with a high concentration of licensed premises was necessary, especially for promoting feelings of safety and reducing fear of crime. Many recounted episodes where they had seen police intervening in disorder or how they felt disorder had been curtailed due to more targeted policing. However, a few felt that on some occasions a high-profile police presence may antagonise the situation, lead people to believe trouble is expected or displace those wishing to cause trouble as they may simply avoid areas with a visible police presence and go elsewhere.

> *Whenever I have noticed a visible police presence it does to an extent make me feel a bit safer*
> (Female, 21-24, northern city)

> *Recently there's always been police outside when we leave and there haven't been that many fights but beforehand you'd get into a fight and generally other people would break it up before the police even got there*
> (Female, 18-20, southern market town)

> *It's probably too obvious, a lot of time during the summer they're wearing the full bright yellow, you can see them a mile off ... if I were going to start a huge fight I'd know where not to go*
> (Female, 21-24, northern city)

There was also some support for the police to deal more harshly with drunken offenders, and for arrestees to have to go through some form of rehabilitation programme to address their alcohol-related offending.

> *I suppose the police could start locking up people, just even for being offensive, just lock them up for a night sort of thing, but I suppose if you did that there's probably not enough cells to go around*
> (Male, 21-24, northern city)

It could be part of the punishment to get them on a course, you know like I have heard of things where victims of crime get the perpetrators to come and talk to them you know listen to their side of the story   (Female, 21-24, northern city)

...before they're allowed to drink again they should have anger management classes
                                                                 (Female, 18-20, northern city)

Get people to start to think next time they go out for a drink, am I drinking too fast I might have a coke next time, you know teach them things like that and maybe give them a kind of curfew or if you get caught again in this period of time you are going to get a harsher penalty   (Female, 21-24, northern city)

Licensed premises

Licensed premises together with the licensed trade were also seen to have a role to play in minimising alcohol-related harm.

Increasingly, licensed premises aimed at the young adult market employ door and security staff to control entrance to the establishment and behaviour within the premises. Whether they adequately fulfilled these roles proved to be contentious. Some thought they did a difficult job well, while others thought they caused more trouble than they prevented. On the whole, door staff seemed to engender negative images, especially among the women interviewed. There was also concern that while door staff may manage incidents in the licensed premises their role only went as far as throwing the people involved into the street, where the violence often continued. Interviewees suggested stricter vetting procedures and intensive training.

I think there should be better vetting definitely cos it seems like anyone can be a bouncer but not everyone has the right mentality. You've got to be quite a strong person to deal with people and alcohol   (Female, 21-24, southern city)

I think there needs to be a tighter rein on them. They need some sort of training or qualification, I just think they need to be trained a bit more on how to treat people
                                                                 (Female, 21-24, northern city)

Interviewees also commented that more staff in licensed premises, both to alleviate the time spent queuing for drinks (seen as resulting in frustrations and potentially arguments and fights) and to monitor activity in the premises, would be helpful.

They don't have enough bar staff for the amount of people at the bar. I think that is probably where you get a lot of aggravation actually at the actual bar especially when it's really busy (Female, 18-20, southern city)

There are never many staff in pubs, you are always fighting for a drink. You get people at the bar and then the rest of the pub has basically got no staff in it so anything could be happening in the corners of the pub which no-one is aware (Female, 21-24, southern city)

There was also widespread support for licensed premises to use plastic bottles (though less support for plastic glasses) in order to reduce injuries associated with glass.

Interviewees felt that changing licensing laws to allow extended opening hours would be beneficial in reducing the intensity of drinking and also the volume of people leaving premises at the same time competing for scarce resources such as taxis or fast food. There was, however, the view that an extension of licensing hours would not have an huge impact on alcohol-related crime as there already exist many late night venues.

If the pub is shutting at 11 you tend to drink a lot in a short space of time, it makes you a lot worse ... I think if places open say 24 hours a day you would see quite a big difference (Male, 21-24, northern city)

Well I would say spread out the hours of drinking ... so that everyone is not going to be on the street at exactly the same time (Female, 18-20, southern market town)

City centres

The interviewees also put forward ideas for improving the safety of busy entertainment districts. These included introduction of safe bottle bins, by-laws banning drinking or use of glass in specified areas, well advertised CCTV cameras and more frequent transport (including night buses) to get people out of entertainment areas at the end of the evening. In areas where some of these initiatives had already begun they were met with enthusiasm.

The buses are pretty horrific but the taxi ranks are awful, you get huge, huge queues of people cutting in and people arguing (Male, 21-24, northern city)

They're very strict about things like taking glass bottles outside ...people generally don't have a problem with it (Female, 21-24, northern city)

Summary

It has previously been established that the young binge drinkers who took part in the in-depth interviews identified alcohol as an influential factor in crime and disorder in and around licensed premises. Following on from this, interviewees were asked for suggestions for reducing alcohol-related offending within the night-time economy. Broadly, ideas fell into two categories, ways of reducing levels of alcohol consumption and ways of reducing crime and disorder. Within these categories key areas for improvement included licensed premises, policing, advertising, education and improvements to city-centre infrastructure. Encouragingly, it was believed that addressing some of the shortcomings of these areas such as increasing transport out of entertainment centres, better targeting of policing and stricter door policies would have a desirable impact on rates of alcohol-related offending and help to make a night out a safer and more enjoyable experience.

7.   Conclusion

This report has examined the extent and nature of binge drinking in the 18- to 24-year-old population and explored links between excessive drinking, crime and disorder and drug use. The nationally representative 1998/1999 Youth Lifestyles Survey provided the statistical basis to explore the links between drinking and, disorder, crime, and drug use, while the in-depth interviews conducted with 18- to 24-year-old binge drinkers explored how young people perceived the relationship between alcohol, crime and illicit drugs. This concluding chapter reflects on some of the findings that are of particular importance in informing policy development.

Binge drinking, crime and disorder

Anecdotally, patterns of so-called 'binge' drinking have often been associated with crime and disorder, particularly that occurring in town and city centres on weekend evenings. This research was designed to explore the extent and nature of this relationship. It should be stated that while the vast majority of 18- to 24-year-olds drink alcohol, the majority do not frequently drink excessively. However, a sizeable minority do, 39 per cent reported getting very drunk at least once a month, and it is this group that the research focuses on.

Is there a relationship between binge drinking, crime and disorder?

Findings from the Youth Lifestyles Survey clearly demonstrate a statistical association between binge drinking and involvement in disorderly or criminal behaviour. While it is not possible to conclude that excessive alcohol consumption per se is causally linked to crime and disorder, the analysis does demonstrate an enduring relationship even after other factors are taken into account. Focusing on incidents of disorder committed during or after drinking, around a third of all 18- to 24-year-olds reported at least one incident. Among binge drinkers this figure rises to 60 per cent.

These findings are important given the relative lack of robust research in this area. They clearly show that young people who engage in binge drinking behaviour are more likely to become involved in crime and disorder, much of which is likely to arise during or immediately following the consumption of alcohol. There could therefore be crime and disorder benefits in reducing such drinking behaviour among young adults, in addition to the health and other social benefits that may arise.

What types of crimes are associated with binge drinking?

Analysis of the Youth Lifestyles Survey confirms that violent crime, while not necessarily widespread, is the offence most strongly associated with binge drinking. Around a quarter of binge drinkers had committed a violent offence during or after drinking alcohol. Moreover, the in-depth interviews indicated that many binge drinkers felt that seeing fights and assaults in and around licensed premises was almost an inevitable part of a weekend night out. While some appeared desensitised to this and could ignore it, it made others feel intimidated and unsafe.

In explaining the links between alcohol and violence, many young people felt that alcohol resulted in increased confidence and disinhibition and this sometimes resulted in aggression and violence. Young people talked about triggers, such as people accidentally bumping into each other, which led to aggressive responses if they had been drinking alcohol.

The links between excessive alcohol consumption and violence are complex. A body of work has explored the nature of the relationship, ranging from the pharmacological impact of alcohol to examination of the social and cultural contexts in which alcohol is consumed (Collins, 1982; Graham et al., 1998). This research does not enable us to fully understand the nature of the relationship. However, given that not every binge drinker commits a disorderly or criminal act it can be safely assumed that there is not a simple direct relationship. Rather a range of individual, environmental and social and cultural factors are all likely to have a role to play.

Are there ways of tackling the problem?

Some commentators may argue that the problem of alcohol-related crime and disorder can not be addressed until the causes are fully identified. However, the young people interviewed suggested many measures that they felt could be taken in an effort to reduce alcohol-related crime and disorder. These were broadly divided into measures to reduce binge drinking and thus reduce the associated harm, though there was some scepticism about the scope to change drinking behaviour among young people, and measures to make the drinking environment safer for those who were drinking. It should be noted that evidence suggests that people are most likely to support measures that will have the least effect upon themselves (Plant and Harrison, 2002). This may be reflected in the fact that many of the interviewees discussed ideas such as advertising campaigns and changes in licensing laws whereas measures such as increase in taxes were not mentioned at all. Also some of the measures put forward such as health education have been found to have limited effect in terms of reducing alcohol use though there is some evidence that they can increase awareness and change attitudes (Plant and Harrison, 2002). Most of the suggestions put forward by young drinkers are consistent with the ideas being promoted by government and other interested stakeholders, including the licensed trade and bodies concerned with alcohol abuse. However, further research would be required to fully identify how effective any of these measures are in practice and furthermore some of the measures may have to be tailored to local circumstances. At present, although there are instances of innovative schemes to address alcohol-related problems, in most cases there is limited evidence as to their effectiveness. A programme in Cardiff, Tackling Alcohol-Related Street Crime (TASC), which has adopted a holistic approach to reduce alcohol-related crime and disorder in two areas of the city, is being evaluated under the Crime Reduction Programme. Results from the 18-month evaluation period while showing a rise in alcohol-related disorder incidents found reductions in physical violence. Moreover, reductions were noted in licensed premises and small areas following targeted policing operations. For a full account of the evaluation see Maguire et al., (forthcoming). It is recommended that where measures are being taken, either nationally or locally, that an important component to consider is an evaluation of effectiveness.

Licensed premises

The interviewees felt that promoting soft drinks at reasonable prices could encourage more moderate drinking. It was also felt that a 'safe drinking' message on bottles would be helpful. Furthermore, displaying the number of units each alcoholic drink contained would aid in self- monitoring of alcohol intake (although concern was expressed that this could be used by some as a way of selecting the stronger drinks). Happy hours and drink promotions were thought to encourage young people to swap drinks, try types of drinks that they usually would not and to drink more alcohol more quickly. While interviewees readily admitted to such promotions increasing their consumption few suggested a ban or restriction on drink promotions as a possible measure to help reduce excessive consumption. This is not to say that such an approach would not be effective. Widespread use of plastic glasses and bottles had some support as a way of reducing injuries from glass.

Staff were seen as key in controlling licensed premises. It was thought that bar staff should not serve intoxicated customers and that more bar staff in busy venues would reduce frustration at the bar, which often led to aggression. Reducing crowding in bars would also seem sensible as pushing others or knocking over drinks was believed to be instrumental in starting confrontations often leading to fights. It was also believed that the role of door staff should include identifying potential problems and quickly preventing fights occurring or escalating. However, many people reported that door staff were unnecessarily aggressive and often exacerbated problems or in some cases were the cause of fights and disorder. Mandatory responsible server training for bar staff and increased training, alongside stricter vetting procedures, for door staff were suggested as ways of addressing these problems.

Outside licensed premises

The remit of door staff is usually to remove trouble from their particular venue often resulting in fights being transferred to the street. Other areas identified as places where disorderly and violent incidents were concentrated were where many young drunk people tended to congregate following a night out, particularly when they were competing for services, for example taxi ranks, bus stops and fast food outlets.

More targeted policing of busy entertainment areas and improved transport links out of centres were thought to be instrumental in improving the safety of areas surrounding licensed premises. Also relaxation of the licensing laws or staggered closing times were viewed positively in terms of reducing the number of people leaving premises en masse at closing time. Other proposed measures included increased, well-advertised CCTV coverage, and safe bottle bins.

Education and advertising

The use of advertising campaigns to convey safe drinking messages and reduce alcohol-related violence met with mixed reactions. Generally the young adults interviewed had not noticed any advertising or campaigns relating to alcohol. Most were sceptical about whether poster campaigns would change people's drinking habits. However, there was a feeling that hard-hitting, carefully placed posters promoting safe drinking messages would be useful. There was more support for a television campaign and many cited the government's drink-driving campaigns as an example of successful advertising that had changed attitudes and behaviour. Alcohol education in schools from a relatively early age met with a lot of support.

Alcohol and illicit drugs

The Youth Lifestyles Survey demonstrated that binge drinkers were far more likely to have taken most types of drugs than other young adults. Again this held even after other factors were taken into account. Furthermore, this report indicates that those who report binge drinking and illegal substance use are more likely to be involved in crime and disorder than those who report only binge drinking or only drug taking. This confirms previous research which has linked illicit and licit substance use and suggests that in addressing either drug use or alcohol use the links between the two need to be fully considered. While the YLS data do not address the issue of the use of alcohol and illicit drugs on the same occasion, the in-depth interviews suggested that cocaine was the drug most commonly used with alcohol, and the use of cocaine was often seen as allowing individuals to drink more. Perhaps as a result of this cocaine was the only illicit drug perceived to be linked to violence in the night-time economy. Overall, the analysis of the YLS showed that while alcohol was most strongly associated with violent crime, drug use was associated with theft.

Table A2.1 *Prevalence and frequency of drinking, by age group and sex*

Percentages	18- to 24-year-olds			25- to 30-year-olds		
	Men	Women	All	Men	Women	All
Had an alcoholic drink (including shandy/alcopops/alcoholic soft/flavoured drinks)						
Ever	97	96	97	96	96	96
Base N (all)	642	715	1357	702	951	1653
In last twelve months	96	93	95	94	92	93
In last 7 days	87	69	78	78	65	71
Base N (all)	628	708	1336	683	929	1612
How often had alcohol in past year						
Just on special occasions	7	13	10	8	17	13
Less than once a month	2	7	4	5	7	6
Once or twice a month	10	13	11	10	14	12
Once a week	20	27	23	21	26	24
2-4 days a week	47	36	41	42	31	36
5-6 days a week	11	5	8	10	4	7
Every day	4	1	2	4	1	2
Number of days in the last week						
None	10	26	18	17	29	23
One	21	21	21	17	24	21
Two	18	20	19	17	20	19
Three	17	14	15	17	11	14
Four	14	10	12	15	8	11
Five	9	7	8	8	4	6
Six	4	1	2	3	1	2
Seven	7	2	4	6	2	4
Base N (those who had drunk in last 12 months)	*603*	*652*	*1255*	*647*	*845*	*1492*

Notes:
1. Source: 1998/1999 Youth Lifestyles Survey.
2. Ever drank questions were asked of respondents with reading problems or where the interviewer read aloud for some other reason. All other questions were self-completed.

Table A2.2   Number and types of alcohol drunk by young adults in the last week, by age group and sex

Percentages	18- to 24-year-olds			25- to 30-year-olds		
	Men	Women	All	Men	Women	All
Types of alcohol drink consumed in the last week						
Drunk beer or lager	94	60	79	95	55	75
Drunk spirits or liqueurs	48	63	55	37	35	36
Drunk wine (including champagne and Babycham)	32	50	40	44	65	54
Drunk alcoholic soft/flavoured drink or alcopop	12	29	20	7	8	7
Drunk cider	9	19	13	8	11	9
Drunk shandy	16	6	12	12	4	8
Drunk other alcoholic drink	9	7	8	8	6	7
Number of types of alcoholic drink consumed in the last week						
One	28	22	26	30	41	35
Two	35	37	36	38	39	38
Three	26	26	26	24	17	21
Four or more	11	15	13	8	3	6
Base N (those who had drunk in last week)	526	470	996	540	580	1120

Notes:
Source: 1998/1999 Youth Lifestyles Survey.

Table A2.3 Number of units of alcohol consumed by young people in last week, by age group and sex

Percentages	18- to 24-year-olds			25- to 30-year-olds		
	Men	Women	All	Men	Women	All
Number of units consumed in last week						
1 to 14	51	73	61	56	86	71
14 to 21	16	15	16	14	8	11
22 to 28	10	6	8	10	4	7
29 to 42	12	4	8	13	1	7
43 to 50	4	1	3	3	<1	2
51 or more	8	2	5	4	1	2
Mean number of units	20.9	12.2	17.0	18.0	8.4	13.4
Base N (those who had drunk in last week)	522	470	992	540	580	1120
None	14	31	22	22	35	29
1 to 14	44	50	47	44	56	50
15 to 21	14	11	12	11	5	8
22 to 28	8	4	6	8	2	5
29 to 42	10	2	6	10	1	5
43 to 50	3	1	2	2	<1	1
51 or more	7	1	4	3	1	2
Mean number of units	18.1	8.4	13.2	14.1	5.5	9.6
Base N (all)	624	708	1332	683	929	1612

Notes:
1. Source: 1998/1999 Youth Lifestyles Survey.
2. In 4 cases the number of units consumed in a week was regarded as too high to be plausible. These have been dropped from the analysis.

Table A2.4 Experiences of drunkenness among young people, by age group and sex

Percentages	18- to 24-year-olds			25- to 30-year-olds		
	Men	Women	All	Men	Women	All
Felt very drunk in the last twelve months						
At least once a week	18	6	12	6	3	4
Several times a month	14	10	12	8	3	6
Once or twice a month	18	17	17	18	8	13
Every couple of months	19	22	21	21	15	18
Less often	15	20	17	26	30	28
Never	16	25	20	21	41	32
Had a hangover in last twelve months						
More than once or twice a week	2	1	1	1	1	<1
About once or twice a week	10	4	7	4	1	2
About once or twice a month	22	14	18	15	6	10
Between three and ten times	15	17	16	21	16	19
Once or twice	21	25	23	28	27	27
Been drunk but never had a hangover	14	14	14	10	9	10
Never been drunk	16	25	20	21	41	32
Base N (those who had drunk last 12 mths)	603	652	1255	647	845	1492

Notes:
1. Source: 1998/1999 Youth Lifestyles Survey.

Table A3.3 Drinking patterns among 18- to 24-year-olds, by binge drinking status

Percentages	Binge drinker	Other regular drinker
Types of alcohol drink consumed in the last week		
Beer or lager	86	75
Cider	16	11
Wine (including champagne and Babycham)	42	39
Spirits or liqueurs	66	46
Alcoholic soft/flavoured drink or alcopop	22	18
Shandy	13	11
Other alcoholic drink	8	8
Base N (those who had drunk in last week)	475	469
Number of types of alcoholic drink in the last week		
One	17	32
Two	33	39
Three	32	21
Four	15	8
Five or more	3	1
Base N (those who had drunk in last week)	475	469
Number of units consumed in last week		
Less than recommended weekly limit	54	84
More than recommended weekly limit	46	16
Mean number of units	23.8	10.7
Base N (those who had drunk in last week)	471	469

Notes:
1. Source: 1998/1999 Youth Lifestyles Survey.

Table A3.4   *Drinking patterns among 18- to 24-year-old binge drinkers, by sex*

Percentages	Binge drinker		Other regular drinker	
	Men	Women	Men	Women
How often had alcohol in past year				
Once or twice a month	2	5	21	23
Once a week	15	24	29	39
2-4 days a week	58	57	43	35
5-6 days a week	16	11	6	2
Every day	7	<1	1	2
Base N (those who had drunk in last 12 months)	*301*	*207*	*246*	*305*
Types of alcohol drink consumed in the last week				
Beer or lager	98	66	93	59
Cider	9	27	9	14
Wine (including champagne and Babycham)	35	53	30	48
Spirits or liqueurs	60	75	33	58
Alcoholic soft/flavoured drink or alcopop	14	34	9	26
Shandy	18	4	15	7
Other alcoholic drink	9	6	9	6
Number of types of alcoholic drink consumed in the last week				
One	21	11	35	28
Two	32	34	39	39
Three	32	33	20	21
Four	13	18	5	12
Five or more	3	3	<1	1
Base N (those who had drunk in last week)	*289*	*186*	*215*	*254*
Number of units consumed in last week				
Less than recommended weekly limit	52	58	85	84
More than recommended weekly limit	48	42	15	16
Mean number of units	27.9	16.9	12.8	8.8
Base N (those who had drunk in last week)	*285*	*186*	*215*	*254*

Notes:
1. Source: 1998/1999 Youth Lifestyles Survey.

Table A3.5   Reasons why drink among 18- to 24-year-olds, by binge drinking status

Percentages	Binge drinker	Other regular drinker	Occasionally/never drinks
To relax			
Agree	72	63	45
Disagree	22	25	38
Don't know	6	12	17
Makes them feel more confident			
Agree	64	54	51
Disagree	28	36	31
Don't know	7	10	17
They like getting drunk			
Agree	86	68	69
Disagree	9	21	13
Don't know	5	10	17
To be sociable with their friends			
Agree	95	91	85
Disagree	4	7	7
Don't know	1	2	8
Like going to pubs and clubs			
Agree	94	91	87
Disagree	5	5	5
Don't know	1	4	8
They are bored/nothing else to do			
Agree	33	24	38
Disagree	59	65	45
Don't know	8	11	17
Base N (all who accepted self-completion)	508	551	277

Notes:
1. Source: 1998/1999 Youth Lifestyles Survey.

Table A3.6 Reasons why drink among 18- to 24-year-old binge drinkers, by sex

Percentages	Binge drinker		Other regular drinker	
	Men	Women	Men	Women
To relax				
Agree	72	72	67	58
Disagree	21	24	22	29
Don't know	7	4	11	12
Makes them feel more confident				
Agree	59	72	52	56
Disagree	33	22	37	35
Don't know	8	6	12	9
They like getting drunk				
Agree	88	83	69	68
Disagree	7	12	17	25
Don't know	5	5	14	7
To be sociable with their friends				
Agree	95	95	89	92
Disagree	5	3	8	6
Don't know	1	2	3	2
Like going to pubs and clubs				
Agree	95	94	90	92
Disagree	5	5	5	4
Don't know	<1	1	4	4
They are bored/have nothing else to do				
Agree	39	23	28	20
Disagree	53	69	60	69
Don't know	8	8	12	11
Base N (all who accepted self-completion)	301	207	246	305

Notes:
1. Source: 1998/1999 Youth Lifestyles Survey.

Table A3.7 Social context of drinking among 18- to 24-year-olds, by binge drinking status

Percentages	Binge drinker	Other regular drinker	Occasionally or never drinks
In last month…			
..went to a pub	95	92	38
..went to party/dance/ nightclub/disco	91	77	44
Base N (all those who accepted self-completion)	508	551	277
Where normally drink			
Pub/wine bar	88	79	48
Own home	33	41	36
Nightclub	46	29	20
Friend's home	9	13	14
At parties	8	8	20
Relative's home	2	5	10
Park or street	1	<1	0
Somewhere else	1	1	1
Who normally drink with			
Friends	96	86	65
Husband/wife/partner/ girl/boyfriend	42	48	49
Parents	13	20	21
Workmates	19	11	9
Brother/sister	1	1	3
Other relatives	<1	1	2
On your own	1	2	2
Someone else	3	3	3
Base N (those who had drunk in last 12 mths)	508	551	196

Notes:
1. Source: 1998/1999 Youth Lifestyles Survey.

Table A3.8   Social context of drinking among 18- to 24-year-old binge drinkers, by sex

Percentages	Binge drinker		Other regular drinker	
	Men	Women	Men	Women
In last month…				
..went to a pub	96	95	92	92
..went to party/dance/nightclub/disco	92	91	77	76
Base N (all those who accepted self-completion)	301	207	246	305
Where normally drink				
Pub/wine bar	88	90	79	79
Nightclub	44	50	33	27
Own home	33	32	39	43
Friend's home	10	8	11	16
At parties	10	4	7	9
Relative's home	2	1	3	6
Park or street	1	0	<1	0
Somewhere else	1	<1	2	1
Who normally drink with				
Friends	96	95	90	82
Husband/wife/partner/girl/boyfriend	42	41	35	59
Parents	12	15	16	24
Workmates	22	14	16	6
Brother/sister	1	1	1	1
Other relatives	1	0	0	1
On your own	1	<1	3	1
Someone else	2	4	3	3
Base N (those who had drunk in last 12 mths)	301	207	246	305

Notes:
1.   Source: 1998/1999 Youth Lifestyles Survey.

Table A4.1   Prevalence of drug use, by age and sex

Percentages	18- to 24-year-olds			25- to 30-year-olds		
	Male	Female	All	Male	Female	All
Cannabis	44	32	38	29	15	21
Amphetamine	21	12	17	9	4	6
Ecstasy	14	5	9	6	1	3
Cocaine	13	5	9	7	2	4
Amyl nitrite	8	3	6	4	>1	2
Mushrooms	7	2	4	4	>1	2
LSD	5	1	3	2	>1	1
Crack	1	0	1	<1	<1	<1
Heroin	2	>1	1	1	0	<1
Any Drug	48	35	41	32	16	24
Base N	617	700	1317	676	918	1594

Notes:
1. Source: 1998/1999 Youth Lifestyles Survey.
2. The base number varied slightly for the different drug types – that shown is for the any drug category.

Table A4.2   Drug use in last 12 months among 18- to 24-year-olds, by binge drinking and sex

Percentages	Binge drinker		Other regular drinker	
	Men	Women	Men	Women
Cannabis	59	48	34	27
Amphetamine	33	22	11	7
Ecstasy	20	9	9	3
Cocaine	19	9	8	4
Amyl nitrite	11	5	6	1
Mushrooms	11	2	2	1
LSD	7	>1	5	2
Crack	2	0	>1	0
Heroin	2	0	2	>1
Any Drug	63	53	36	29
Base N	296	204	242	304

Notes:
1. Source: 1998/1999 Youth Lifestyles Survey.
2. The base number varied slightly for the different drug types – that shown is for the any drug category.

Table A4.3   Predictive factors for 18- to 24-year-olds – drug use

Exp(β)	Any Drug	Cannabis	Amphetamine	Cocaine	Ecstasy
Frequency of drinking (base: less than once a month)					
At least once a week	2.16 *	2.09 *	ns	ns	ns
Once or twice a month	1.51	1.59	ns	ns	ns
Frequency of drunkenness (base: less than once a month)					
At least once a week	3.61 *	3.39 *	5.18 *	4.89 *	3.04 *
Once or twice a month	2.47 *	2.43 *	3.25 *	3.17 *	3.91 *
Visiting pub/club in last month					
Yes	ns	ns	ns	8.24 *	ns
Employment (base: working)					
Studying	ns	ns	0.41 *	ns	0.49 *
Other	ns	ns	1.14	ns	1.31
Unemployed	ns	ns	1.26	ns	1.91 *
Qualifications (base: higher)					
Other	0.97	ns	5.59 *	6.93 *	ns
None	0.60	ns	1.99	3.15 *	ns
GCSE	1.23	ns	2.17 *	2.02	ns
A levels	1.33	ns	2.99 *	3.00 *	ns
Housing tenure (base: owner occupier)					
Other	0.86	0.89	1.58	0.81	1.35
Privately renting	2.08 *	2.03 *	2.43 *	2.55 *	2.72 *
Social housing	1.33	1.16	1.28	0.75	0.58
Other factors					
Male	1.40 *	1.30 *	1.51 *	2.04 *	2.18 *
18-20	ns	ns	ns	0.48 *	ns
White	1.79 *	ns	5.95 *	ns	ns
No children	ns	1.56 *	ns	ns	ns
Single	ns	ns	ns	ns	2.40 *
Expelled/excluded from school	3.86 *	3.22 *	2.51 *	3.96 *	3.47 *
Hosmer and Lemeshow	#	#	#	#	#
Base N:	1296	1299	1300	1305	1308

Notes:
1. * indicates statistic is significant; ns indicates the variable was not significant in any of the models.
2. # indicates Hosmer and Lemeshow test is not significant i.e. model is a good fit.
3. The variable spending money was also tested but did not come out in the model.

Table A5.1 Offending among young adults, by sex and age

Percentages	18- to 24-year-olds			25- to 30-year-olds		
	Men	Women	All	Men	Women	All
Any offence in last 12 months	33	13	23	20	7	13
Violent crime	15	2	8	3	1	2
Taken part in a group fight in public place	13	1	8	2	<1	1
Theft	12	4	8	5	1	2
Criminal damage	4	<1	2	1	<1	<1
Base N	444	473	917	641	889	1530

Notes:
1. Source: 1998/1999 Youth Lifestyles Survey.

Table A5.2 Offending among 18- to 24-year-olds, by binge drinking status

Percentages	Binge Other regular drinker	Occasionally drinker	or never drinks
Any offence in last 12 months	39	14	8
Violent crime	17	4	2
Taken part in a group fight in public place	15	3	2
Theft	11	6	3
Criminal damage	4	<1	1
Base N	355	381	181

Notes:
1. Source: 1998/1999 Youth Lifestyles Survey.

Table A5.3   Offending among 18- to 24-year-olds, by binge drinking and sex

Percentages	Binge drinker		Other regular drinker	
	Men	Women	Men	Women
Any offence in last 12 months	49	22	21	8
Violent crime	25	3	7	1
Taken part in a group fight in public place	22	2	6	1
Theft	16	4	10	3
Criminal damage	7	<1	1	0
Base N	212	143	176	205

Notes:
1. Source: 1998/1999 Youth Lifestyles Survey.

Table A5.4   Offending in the last 12 months – predictive factors for 18- to 24-year-olds

Exp(β)	Any Offence	Violent Crime	Fighting	Theft
Frequency of Drunkenness (base: less than once a month)				
At least once a week	3.02 *	5.63 *	5.74 *	ns
Once or twice a month	1.95 *	3.12 *	2.85 *	ns
Other factors				
Male	2.83 *	6.83 *	6.62 *	3.87 *
Know delinquent	2.39 *	3.31 *	2.78 *	3.03 *
Expelled/excluded	ns	2.04 *	ns	ns
Used a drug in last twelve months	4.02 *	ns	ns	2.36 *
Hosmer and Lemeshow	#	#	#	#
Base N	867	867	867	867

Notes:
1. Source: 1998/1999 Youth Lifestyles Survey.
2. * indicates statistic is significant; ns indicates the variable was not significant.
3. # indicates Hosmer and Lemeshow test is not significant therefore model is a good fit.
4. Employment status, ethnicity, marital status, children, educational qualifications, amount of spending money, frequency of drinking and going to pubs or clubs did not come out in the model.

Table A5.5   Crime and disorder while drinking, by sex and age

Percentages	18- to 24-year-olds			25- to 30-year-olds		
	Men	Women	All	Men	Women	All
In the past 12 months has during or after drinking …						
…got into a heated argument	41	24	33	23	14	18
…got into a fight	23	5	14	9	2	6
…broken, destroyed or damaged something belonging to someone else	14	3	9	4	1	2
…taken something belonging to someone else	7	1	4	1	1	1
…done any of the above	50	26	38	26	16	21
Base N (those who had drunk last 12 mths)	603	652	1255	647	845	1492

Notes:
1. Source: 1998/1999 Youth Lifestyles Survey.

Table A5.6   Crime and disorder while drinking among 18- to 24-year-olds, by drinking status

Percentages	Binge drinker	Other regular drinker	Occasionally drinks[2]
In the past 12 months has during or after drinking …			
…got into a heated argument	50	23	12
…got into a fight	26	7	3
…broken, destroyed or damaged something belonging to someone else	17	3	1
…taken something belonging to someone else	8	1	1
…done any of the above	60	25	13
Base N (those who had drunk last 12 mths)	508	551	196

Notes:
1. Source: 1998/1999 Youth Lifestyles Survey.
2. Drunk alcohol less than once a month in the previous twelve months.

Table A5.7 **Crime and disorder while drinking among 18- to 24-year-olds, by binge drinking and sex**

Percentages	Binge drinker		Other regular drinker	
	Men	Women	Men	Women
In the past 12 months has during or after drinking ...				
...got into a heated argument	56	41	30	18
...got into a fight	35	11	12	2
...broken, destroyed or damaged something belonging to someone else	23	7	6	2
...taken something belonging to someone else	12	2	1	1
...done any of the above	69	45	34	18
Base N (those who had drunk last 12 mths)	301	207	246	305

Notes:
1. Source: 1998/1999 Youth Lifestyles Survey.

Table A5.8 Consequences of drinking - predictive factors for 18- to 24-year-olds

Exp(β)	Any consequence	Heated argument	Got into a fight	Broken, damaged
Frequency of drinking (base: less than once a month)				
At least once a week	1.98 *	ns	ns	ns
Once or twice a month	1.64	ns	ns	ns
Frequency of drunkenness (base: less than once a month)				
At least once a week	4.33 *	3.79 *	5.02 *	6.80 *
Once or twice a month	3.09 *	3.03 *	3.27 *	3.18 *
Age of first drink (base: 15-24)				
1-twelve	1.46 *	1.60 *	ns	ns
13-14	1.76 *	1.87 *	ns	ns
Qualifications (base: higher)				
Other	ns	ns	8.18 *	ns
None	ns	ns	4.42 *	ns
GCSE	ns	ns	1.11	ns
A levels	ns	ns	1.38	ns
Other factors				
Male	2.08 *	1.64 *	4.33 *	3.93 *
18-20	ns	ns	2.32 *	ns
Used a drug	1.75 *	1.81 *	2.58 *	3.01 *
Hosmer and Lemeshow	#	#	#	#
Base N	1237	1237	1237	1237

Notes:
1. Source: 1998/1999 Youth Lifestyles Survey.
2. *indicates statistic is significant; ns indicates the variable was not significant.
3. # indicates Hosmer and Lemeshow test is not significant therefore model is a good fit.
4. Employment status ethnicity, children, marital status, going to a pub or club and going out in the evening were also tested but did not come out in the model.

Appendix B   Binge drinking: definitions and findings

Survey	Sample for the figures presented here	Definition of binge drinking	% defined as binge drinkers	% young people defined as binge drinkers
Drinking: adults' behaviour and knowledge in 2000 (ONS Omnibus)	Great Britain adults aged 16 and over	8+ /6+ units (men/women) at least one day in previous week	All men = 20% All women = 8%	16-24 men = 38% 16-24 women = 25%
Living in Britain (Results from the 2000/2001 General Household Survey)	Great Britain adults aged 16 and over	8+/6+ units (men/women) at least one day in previous week	All men = 21% All women = 10%	16-24 men = 37% 16-24 women = 27%
The Health Survey for adults England 1998	England aged 16 and over	8+/6+ units at least one day in the previous week	Those who drank in last week men = 33% women = 19%	Those who drank in last week 16-24 men = 58% 16-24 women = 38%
The Health Survey for England: Health of Young People 95-97	England 16-24 year olds	Slightly or very drunk at least once a week in the past 3 months	Not applicable	16-24 men = 34% 16-24 women = 19%

Appendix C

The study is based on two sources of data: the 1998/1999 Youth Lifestyles Survey and in-depth interviews conducted with 27 young adults in late 2001/early 2002. Each source of data is discussed below.

The Youth Lifestyles Survey

The 1998/99 Youth Lifestyles Survey is a nationally representative survey of 4,848 12- to 30-year-olds living in private households in England and Wales.[18] The sample for the 1998/99 survey was generated from the 1998 British Crime Survey (BCS) sample.[19] The overall response rate was 69 per cent. The survey was conducted between October 1998 and January 1999 by the National Centre for Social Research (formerly SCPR).

The survey was primarily designed to provide a national estimate of self-reported offending by 12- to 30-year-olds. However, it also collected basic socio-demographic details and information about respondents' lifestyles, including their use of alcohol and illicit drugs.

Respondents were interviewed in their own home by interviewers using Computer Assisted Interviewing. Questions on alcohol, drug use and offending behaviour were asked by self-completion, using Computer Assisted Self-Interviewing, because of their sensitive nature.

Weights were applied to the data to take into account different sampling rates introduced by the sample design and to adjust for non-response. Results presented in this report are based on weighted data.

As with any household survey, the YLS findings are subject to sampling error and a range of other methodological limitations, such as non-response bias, coverage being limited to private households, and the ability of respondents to interpret questions as intended and to be willing and able to provide accurate answers.

- Coverage – young people in institutions are likely to be more deviant in alcohol, drugs and offending and are not included in the YLS sample.

18. Note that the 1998/1999 was the second sweep of the survey. The first sweep was conducted in 1993 (Graham and Bowling, 1995).
19. 3,643 respondents were interviewed from households in the BCS sampling frame, 1,205 were interviewed in households next to BCS sampled addresses.

- Non-response – it is possible that non-response may be higher in the deviant population. Some weighting of the data was undertaken to correct for non-response (see technical report for further details).
- Willing and able to respond accurately – in an effort to overcome problems of social desirability the YLS used a self-completion format for the most sensitive questions. However, some respondents may still have been unwilling to admit to certain behaviours. Also some respondents may have had difficulty accurately recalling their own behaviour. It is also possible that people who are willing to admit to certain behaviours are also willing to admit to others and this could inflate the correlation between alcohol use and offending.

A more detailed account of the methodology can be found in Flood-Page et al., 2000. The full technical report details the sampling strategy and includes a copy of the questionnaire (Stratford and Roth, 1999).

Analysis of the YLS

For the purposes of this study we were interested primarily in the 18- to 24-year-old age group (n=1,334)[20], though comparisons were made with 25- to 30-year-olds where relevant (n=1,608)[21]. Those aged from 12 to 17 were excluded from the analysis because it was felt that underage drinking was a separate issue (see Harrington, 2000 for findings on underage drinking). Table C.1 gives the socio-demographic profile of the sample.

---

20. This figure refers to only those who accepted self completion. n=1376 for all 18- to 24-year-olds in the sample eligible for self-completion.
21. This figure refers only to those who accepted self-completion. n=1682 for all 25- to 30-year-olds in the sample eligible for self-completion.

Table C.1 Socio-demographic profile of respondents

Percentage	Male 18-24	Female 18-24	Male 25-30	Female 25-30
Ethnicity				
White	94	92	92	92
Black	1	2	2	3
Asian	3	4	4	4
Other	2	3	3	1
Occupation				
At school	3	2	0	0
Higher education	18	22	4	2
Training	2	>1	0	0
Working	65	53	93	68
Unemployed	10	6	4	6
Other	2	15	3	23
Marital status				
Single	89	78	42	33
Married/cohabiting	11	21	57	60
Divorced/separated/ widowed	0.5	2	2	7
Parental status				
Has children	7	22	32	52
Base (those who accepted self-completion)	628	706	682	926

1. Percentages may not add up to 100 due to rounding.

The YLS provided two alternative approaches to defining binge drinking.

The first definition was based on unit-consumption in the week prior to interview. All those who had consumed alcohol in the seven days before interview were asked (a) on how many days they had drunk alcohol and (b) the number of standard drinks consumed of each type of beverage asked about in the previous week. The total number of units consumed was calculated for each respondent using the following calculation:

- Half a pint, a bottle or can of beer, lager or shandy ➜ 1 unit
- Glass of wine ➜ 1 unit

- Single measure of spirits or liqueurs ➜ 1 unit
- Bottle or can of alcopop ➜ 1.5 units
- Other alcoholic drink ➜ 1 unit

This figure was then divided by the number of days in which the person had drunk in the past week to give the average number of units per day. The results were examined to decide upon a suitable cut-off point for binge drinkers and non-binge drinkers. Given the need to have a sufficient number of binge drinkers for further analysis, it was decided to adopt the definition used in other national surveys *men who had drunk more than eight units on at least one day in the past week and women who had drunk more than six units on at least one day in the past week.*

Apart from the inherent difficulties in asking people to recall their alcohol consumption, even over a relatively short period of time, and assuming standard unit definitions despite the range in strengths of different 'brands' of alcoholic drink, this unit-based definition also has other difficulties. It will underestimate the proportion of binge drinkers as some drinkers may have had more to drink on some days than others. For example, a male consuming twelve units over two days would not be classified as a binge drinker based on an average of six units per drinking day. However, he may have consumed ten units on one day and two on the other. Furthermore, this approach does not pick up the respondents who may binge drink but had not done so in the last week and provides no indication of the frequency of binge drinking.

The second definition was based on frequency of drunkenness. All those who had drunk alcohol in the previous twelve months were asked *'How often have you felt very drunk in the last twelve months?'*. Those who responded *At least once a week, Several times a month* or *Once or twice a month* were classified as binge drinkers. This definition overcame many of the problems of the unit-based definition. However, it should be noted that different individuals may have different views as to what constitutes being 'very drunk' as opposed to say just a little drunk.

Analysis was undertaken using both definitions. The results indicated that patterns of offending behaviour were similar for both definitions. However, it was decided that the drunkenness definition was a better measure of binge drinking partly because it captures the frequency of behaviour over a period of twelve months and thus reflects typical behaviour. In addition, it may be that drunkenness itself is a better definition of intoxication than the unit-based measure because it takes into account individual differences.

All significant differences presented in the report are significant at least at the two-tailed ten per cent level.

In-depth interviews

The YLS provided a useful source to quantitatively examine the association between binge drinking, offending and drug use. However, to try and more fully understand the nature of this association and young people's motivations for binge drinking it was necessary to conduct in-depth, qualitative interviews with a sample of young people. In total 27 young people aged from 18 to 24 were interviewed. The sample was selected from nine licensed premises in three town and city centres across England. The locations were:

- an affluent town in southern England with a thriving entertainment area in the town centre, comprising a range of popular chain bars and pubs and several nightclubs;
- a large, vibrant city centre in the North West; and

- a heavily populated suburb of a large south-eastern city.

Once the areas had been identified contact was made with representatives in each police force. Through discussions with police officers and observational visits to pubs and bars, between two and four premises were identified in each location. It was decided not to include nightclubs in this study (see Deehan, forthcoming for a discussion of substance taking in nightclubs). All of the selected establishments were premises that particularly attracted young people. Licensees of these premises were contacted directly to seek access to their premises for a Friday or Saturday evening for the distribution of a short self-completion questionnaire. All licensees agreed to participate in the research. A questionnaire was distributed to clientele considered to be in the 18- to 24-year-old age range by the fieldworkers. Fieldwork took place between 7p.m. and 10p.m. The questionnaire collected information to inform the selection of a suitable sub-sample for follow-up in-depth interviews. Respondents were asked for basic socio-demographic details and information about their drinking patterns and experiences of disorderly and criminal behaviour during or after drinking. The questionnaire made it clear the information was being collected in confidence. At the end of the questionnaire respondents were instructed to indicate whether they were content to be contacted again to take part in an interview and if so to provide their contact details.

Individuals for the in-depth interviews were selected on the basis of their responses to the short questionnaire. The aim was to select those who were binge drinkers and had been very drunk at least once in the past year. Overall, 189 respondents met the criteria for re-contact (i.e., aged from 18 to 24, classified as binge drinkers and answering yes to at least one questions about criminal or disorderly behaviour). Of these, 102 had agreed to be re-contacted. In total 27 respondents were interviewed. The demographic breakdown was as follows; ten male, seventeen female; fourteen 18- to 20-year-olds, thirteen 21- to 24-year-olds; twelve from a northern city, nine from a southern city, six from a southern market town; fourteen working and thirteen in education.

The interviews took place in a location close to where the participant was recruited. All interviews took place during the day or early evening. All interviews were audio-taped, with the permission of the respondent, and transcribed verbatim. Interviews lasted on average 45 minutes.

Although the interviews were not intended to be prescriptive, all researchers used an interview schedule which outlined the topic areas and particular issues that were to be covered in each interview. The interview schedule was based around four main headings:

- *The social context of drinking* – concentrating on what the participant did on a typical night out – drinking patterns, rituals around drinking and the preparation for drinking, what and with whom they drank and the use of illegal drugs in combination with alcohol.
- *Attitudes towards drinking* – attitudes and opinions about alcohol, binge drinking, their own drinking behaviour and illicit drugs.
- *Knowledge of alcohol* – awareness of sensible drinking guidelines/campaigns, harmful effects of alcohol, ideas for interventions.
- *Experiences while intoxicated* – the individual's experience of harmful effects of alcohol, particularly experiences of crime and disorder, whether as a victim, perpetrator, or witness.

Analysis of the in-depth interviews was aided through the use of a qualitative analysis software package. A coding frame, based on the analysis of the Youth Lifestyles Survey, the topic guide and other interesting and relevant themes that emerged out of the interviews, was decided prior to the analysis. All of the transcripts were entered into the package, coded and then manipulated using the search facilities.

References

Aitken, P.P. and Jahoda, G. (1983) An observational study of young adults' drinking groups: I. Drink preferences, demographic and structural variables as predictors of alcohol consumption, *Alcohol & Alcoholism,* 18: 135-150.

Borges, G., Cherpital, C. J. and Rosovsky, H. (1998) Male drinking and violence-related injury in the emergency room, *Addiction* 93(1), 103-1twelve.

Budd, T. and Sims, L. (2001) *Antisocial behaviour: findings from the 2000 British Crime Survey.* Research Findings No. 145. London: Home Office.

Casswell, S., Zhang, J.F. and Wyllie, A. (1993) The importance of amount and location of drinking for the experience of alcohol-related problems, *Addiction,* 88, 1527-1534.

Cherpitel, C. J. (1993) Alcohol and violence-related injuries: an emergency room study, *Addiction,* 88, 79-88.

Collins, J.J. Jr. (1982) *Drinking and Crime: Perspectives on the Relationship between Alcohol Consumption and Criminal Behaviour.* London: Tavistock.

Corkery, J. (2001) *Drug Seizure and Offender Statistics, United Kingdom, 1999.* Statistical Bulletin 5/01. London: Home Office.

Deehan, A. and Saville, E. (forthcoming) *Calculating the risk: Recreational drug use among clubbers in the South East of England.* London: Home Office.

Deehan, A., Marshall, E. and Saville, E. (2002) *Drunks and disorder: a description of alcohol-related crime and disorder in two late night city centres,* Police Research Series Paper 150. London: Home Office.

Deehan, A. and Saville, E. (1999) *Alcohol and Crime: Taking stock.* Crime Reduction Series Paper 3. London: Home Office.

Engineer, R., Phillips, A., Thompson, J. and Nicholls, J. (2003) *Drunk and disorderly: a qualitative study of binge drinking among 18- 24-year-olds,* Home Office Research Study 262. London: Home Office.

Felson, M., Berends, R., Richardson, B. and Veno, A. (1997) Reducing Pub Hopping and Related Crime, in Homel, R. (ed) *Policing for Prevention: Reducing Crime, Public Intoxication and Injury.* New York: Criminal Justice Press.

Finney, A. (forthcoming) *Violence in the night-time economy: key findings from research.* London: Home Office.

Flood-Page, C., Campbell, S., Harrington, V. and Miller, J. (2000) *Youth crime: Findings from the 1998/99 Youth Lifestyles Survey,* Home Office Research Study 209. London: Home Office.

Gilbert, M.J. (1990) The anthropologist as alcohologist: Qualitative perspectives and methods in alcohol research, *International Journal of the Addictions,* 25(2), 127-147.

Graham K., Leonard, K.E., Room, R., Wild, C., Pihl, R.O., Bois, C. and Single, E. (1998) Current directions in research on understanding and preventing intoxicated aggression. *Addiction,* 93 (5), 659-676.

Graham, J. and Bowling, B. (1995) *Young people and crime,* Home Office Research Study No 145, London: HMSO

Harrington, V. (2000) *Underage Drinking: Findings from the 1998-9 Youth Lifestyles Survey,* Research Findings No. 125. London: Home Office.

Homel, R., McIlwain, G. and Carvolth, R. (2001) Creating Safer Drinking Environments, in Heather, N., Peters, T. J. and Stockwell, T. (eds) *International Handbook of Alcohol Dependence and Problems.* Chichester: John Wiley and Sons Ltd.

Honess, T., Seymour, L. and Webster, R. (2000) *The social contexts of underage drinking.* Occasional Paper. London: Home Office.

Kershaw, C., Budd, T., Kinshott, G., Mattinson, J., Mathew, P. and Myhill, A. (2000) *The British Crime Survey England and Wales, 2000,* London: Home Office.

MacAskill, S., Cooke, E., Eadie, D. and Hastings, G. (2001) *Perceptions of factors that protect against the misuse of alcohol amongst young people and young adults.* http://www.scotland.gov.uk/library3/social/pfaa-00.asp

Maguire, M., Nettleton, H., Rix, A. and Raybould, S. (forthcoming) *Reducing Alcohol-Related Violence and Disorder: An Evaluation of the 'TASC' Project.* London: Home Office.

Marlatt, G. A., Baer, J.S., and Larimer, M. (1995) Preventing alcohol abuse in college students; a harm reduction approach, in Boyd, G., Howard J. and Zucker, R. (eds) *Alcohol Problems Amongst Adolescents. UK: Hove.*

Mattinson, J. (2001) *Stranger and Acquaintance Violence: Practice Messages from the British Crime Survey.* Briefing Note 7/01. London: Home Office.

Measham, F., Aldridge, J. and Parker, H. (2001) *Dancing on Drugs: risk, health and hedonism in the British club scene.* London: Free Association Press.

Measham, F. (1996) The 'big bang' approach to sessional drinking: changing patterns of alcohol consumption amongst young people in north west England. *Addiction Research 4,* 283-299.

Midanik, L.T. (1999) Drunkenness, feeling the effects and 5+ measures. *Addiction,* 94(6), 887-897.

Moore, L., Smith, C. and Catford, J. (1994) Binge drinking: prevalence patterns and policy, *Health Education Research,* 9, 497-505.

Murgraff, V., Parrott, A., and Bennett, P. (1999) Risky Single-Occasion Drinking Amongst Young People–Definition, Correlates, Policy, and Intervention: A Broad Overview of Research Findings, *Alcohol & Alcoholis,* 34(1), 3-14.

National Centre for Social Research (1998) *Health Survey for England: the health of young people '95-97 a survey carried out on behalf of The Department of Health,* London: HMSO.

Newburn, T. and Shiner, M. (2001) *Teenage Kicks? Young people and alcohol: A review of the literature.* Joseph Rowntree Foundation.

Nezlak, J.B., Pilkington, C.J. and Bilbro, K.G. (1994) Moderation in excess: binge drinking and social interaction amongst college students, *Journal of Studies on Alcohol,* 55, 342-351.

Office for National Statistics (ONS) (1998) *General Household Survey,* London: HMSO.

Pearson, G. (1998) *Normal Risks: an ethnographic study of adults' recreational drug use in inner London.* Conference paper, 9th Annual Conference on Drug Use and Drug Policy, Palma, Spain.

Parker, H., Aldridge, J. and Measham, F. (1998) *Illegal Leisure. The normalization of adolescent recreational drug use.* London: Routledge.

Pernanen, K. (1991) *Alcohol in Human Violence.* New York: Guilford Press.

Plant, M. and Harrison, L. (2002) Research into harm minimisation related to alcohol problems in Alcohol Concern, *100% Proof: Research for Action on Alcohol.* London: Alcohol Concern.

Ramsey, M., Baker, P., Goulden, C., Sharp, C. and Sondhi, A. (2001) *Drug misuse declared in 2000: results from the British Crime Survey.* Home Office Research Study 224. London: Home Office.

Raistrick, D., Hodgson, R. and Ritson, B. (eds) (1999) *Tackling Alcohol Together,* London: Free Association Press.

Rehm, J., Ashley, M.J., Room, R., Single, E., Bondy, S., Ferrence, R., and Giesbrecht, N. (1996) On the Emerging Paradigm of Drinking Patterns and their Social and Health Consequences, *Addiction,* 91(11), 1615-1621.

Royal College of Physicians. (2001) *Alcohol – can the NHS afford it? Recommendations for a coherent alcohol strategy for hospitals.* London: Royal College of Physicians.

Saunders, P. (1998) The good practice of the police: an alternative approach in dealing with offenders who abuse/misuse alcohol, *Alcohol and Alcoholism,* 43(1), 73-77.

Shepherd, J. and Brickley, M. (1996) The relationship between alcohol intoxication, stressors and injury in urban violence. *British Journal of Criminology,* 36(4), 546-566.

Stratford, N. and Roth, W. (1999) The 1998 Youth Lifestyles Survey. Technical Report. London: National Centre for Social Research.

Webb, E., Ashton, C.H., Kelly, P. and Karnali F. (1996) Alcohol and Drug Use in UK University Students, *The Lancet,* 348, 922-925.

Wechsler, H., Lee, J.E., Kuo, M., Lee, H. (2000) College Binge Drinking in the 1990s: A Continuing Problem, *Journal of American College Health* 48, 199-210.

Wechsler, H., Dowdall, G., Davenport, A. and Rimm, E.B. (1995) A gender-specific measure of binge drinking among college students, American Journal of Public Health, 85, 982-985.

RDS Publications

Requests for Publications

Copies of our publications and a list of those currently available may be obtained from:

Home Office
Research, Development and Statistics Directorate
Communication Development Unit
Room 275, Home Office
50 Queen Anne's Gate
London SW1H 9AT
Telephone: 020 7273 2084 (answerphone outside of office hours)
Facsimile: 020 7222 0211
E-mail: publications.rds@homeoffice.gsi.gov.uk

alternatively

why not visit the RDS website at
    Internet: http://www.homeoffice.gov.uk/rds/index.html

where many of our publications are available to be read on screen or downloaded for printing.